INVEST
NOW

INVEST NOW

A Canadian's Guide to Investing

A. Dawn

Creator of Canada's Personal Finance Website

iUniverse, Inc.
New York Lincoln Shanghai

INVESTNOW
A Canadian's Guide to Investing

Copyright © 2008 by A. Dawn

All rights reserved. No part of this book may be used or reproduced by any means, graphic, electronic, or mechanical, including photocopying, recording, taping or by any information storage retrieval system without the written permission of the publisher except in the case of brief quotations embodied in critical articles and reviews.

iUniverse books may be ordered through booksellers or by contacting:

iUniverse
2021 Pine Lake Road, Suite 100
Lincoln, NE 68512
www.iuniverse.com
1-800-Authors (1-800-288-4677)

Because of the dynamic nature of the Internet, any Web addresses or links contained in this book may have changed since publication and may no longer be valid.

The information, ideas, and suggestions in this book are not intended to render professional advice. Before following any suggestions contained in this book, you should consult your personal accountant or other financial advisor. Neither the author nor the publisher shall be liable or responsible for any loss or damage allegedly arising as a consequence of your use or application of any information or suggestions in this book.

ISBN: 978-0-595-46132-5 (pbk)
ISBN: 978-0-595-70286-2 (cloth)
ISBN: 978-0-595-90433-4 (ebk)

Printed in the United States of America

This book is dedicated to the Canadian soldiers deployed in Afghanistan and other countries abroad. Your courage and hard work are an inspiration to all of us.

Money is like a sixth sense—and you can't make use of the other five without it.

—*William Somerset Maugham*

Contents

Preface xi
Introduction. xiii
Chapter 1   The First Thing You Need to Know. 1
Chapter 2   Why Keeping Money in a Bank Account
            Is Not Good Enough 7
Chapter 3   You Don't Have to Be a Financial Guru
            to Start Investing 10
Chapter 4   Financial Markets. 12
Chapter 5   Financial Products 21
Chapter 6   Mutual Funds: The First-Time
            Investor's Friend. 28
Chapter 7   Advantages of Mutual Funds 30
Chapter 8   Disadvantages of Mutual Funds 35
Chapter 9   Fees and Expenses. 37
Chapter 10 Types of Funds. 45
Chapter 11 The Easy Portfolio 51

Chapter 12	Start Investing Now, Option A: Walk into a Bank........................56
Chapter 13	Start Investing Now, Option B: Make a Phone Call........................59
Chapter 14	Start Investing Now, Option C: Open a Trading Account....................61
Chapter 15	Cool Research Tools..................65
Chapter 16	ING Direct Mutual Funds............70
Chapter 17	Index Funds........................73
Chapter 18	I Don't Have Money to Invest.........75
Chapter 19	Investment Scams: Use Common Sense to Protect Your Money................79
Chapter 20	Tax and Investments.................88
Chapter 21	Canada's Personal Finance Web Site.....96
Chapter 22	A Dawn Journal....................103

Afterword..111
Conclusion...115
Resources..119
Index..129

Preface

Every day, we face tempting opportunities to spend money. A sea of indulgences can distract you from investing for your future. "Buy now!" "Pay after one year!" "Don't pay interest for six months!" Everyone everywhere is urging you to spend, spend, spend. I've even seen a "Vacation now, pay later!" advertisement on the subway. But every dollar you spend now is a dollar in lost investment opportunities that could have grown a lot more in the long run.

Most Canadians were never taught any personal-finance lessons in school and in university; it is no wonder our savings rate is one of the lowest among industrialized nations. To make things worse, Statistics Canada reports that our average savings rate went below zero for the first time in 2006. This is scary—why is it happening?

Our main problem is a lack of information. Also, we have this idea that in order to invest, we need a lot of money, a PhD, and status as an investment guru. In this book, I will show you how you can start investing with very little money—and even less expertise. Investing can be as simple as walking into a bank or picking up your phone.

Start investing today toward a better future. No one else will do it for you; this is *your* future, and *your* investment decisions will have enormous impact. Don't wait until tomorrow, or next month, or next year. Do it now. This is the time.

Introduction

Why This Book?

If you walk down the personal-finance aisle in a bookstore like Chapters, you will find thousands of finance books covering a wide range of topics. These books will promise to share the secrets of millionaires: how to make millions working on the weekends, how to retire as a millionaire, how to make millions in real estate, how to be rich within a few months ... it goes on and on. If you've never invested before, you will leave the bookstore even more confused than when you started.

All of those books have something in common: they aren't for amateurs. Hardly any books on that shelf will stick to the basics, much less provide a step-by-step starter guide. What kind of account should you open? Where should you go to do that? What research is required? What investments are ideal for those of modest means? You may not find the answers to those questions on the bookstore shelves, but you will find them here. I have answered those questions and more in a very simple way. Read, do your research, and start investing.

Why We Never Invest

Ten years ago, I earned my degree in economics, and I have worked in the financial industry ever since. Such a career has many advantages; I really enjoy being able to help friends and family with questions they hesitate to ask anyone else. No one wants to be the person peppering a complete stranger with questions that may seem stupid, so they come to me.

It's just not my friends and family. Most Canadians are in the same situation. They work hard, earn their money, and content themselves with the minimal to nonexistent interest they are getting from their bank accounts. This has to change. You don't have to be a loaded financial genius to invest. All you need is the right information, and that is why I created my first Web site, www.adawn.net: to make the world of personal finance accessible to Canadians. This book will teach you all the basics you need to become a successful investor, and www.adawn.net, *Canada's Personal Finance Web Site*, can give you that extra push toward success.

A Failure in Education

Our education system does not teach how to handle our own money. Usually, we learn it from our friends, our families and from our own mistakes. And the results are obvious: most of us enter the workforce without knowing anything about managing money and investments. If, like many others, you never thought of investing, the simple language of this book will help you invest successfully on your own.

This Book Is Not for You If ...

If you want to become a millionaire overnight or are praying for some other financial miracle, this book is not for you. As I will mention repeatedly, investment is an art. As such, it requires discipline, hard work and consistency. I don't believe in making quick bucks without hard work, and I don't enjoy anything that comes easy. In my book or on my Web site, I will not recommend or review any risky products promising to make you a millionaire (such as penny stocks). In fact, I will ask you to stay away from such products.

This Book Is for You If ...

If you have always wondered whether is it possible to invest without being rich, this book is for you. If you have always wanted to invest but are not sure how to start, this book is for you. If you have just finished school and entered the workforce, this book is for you. If you are a hard-working Canadian and want more value for your money, this book is for you. If you want a better future tomorrow by working hard today, this book is for you.

Frequently Asked Questions

I have tried to answer some of the most common questions you may have regarding this book. Introductions do not usually feature an FAQ section, but I thought, why not give it a try?

- **Who are you?**

    I come from a strong financial background. My extensive education, training and experience have enabled me to develop the knowledge and skills required to write this book and run two popular personal-finance Web sites.

- **Why is this book so thin?**

    Are fat books better than thin ones? I don't think so. I have eliminated chitchat, small talk and stories of John and Jane, organizing this book with only the stuff you need to know. I could have made this a 300-page book, if I valued quantity over quality. But that wouldn't help beginners invest any more wisely. All of the information you need is here.

- **I don't have money; how can I invest?**

    Contrary to popular belief, you don't need a lot of money to invest. This book teaches how to start investing with a small amount, such as $25.

- **Why can't you just tell me what to buy?**

    Every individual is different. What is right for you may not be right for someone else. Rather than recommending specific funds, this book provides all the tools and information necessary for finding what is right for you.

- **OK, I think the tools and information provided here are great, but I'm still not ready to act on my own.**

    That's OK. This book covers several techniques. Following any one will make you a successful investor. If you are not ready to invest on your own, follow the procedures mentioned in this book to obtain advice from a financial advisor without paying any fees.

Chapter 1

The First Thing You Need to Know

Let the Journey Begin

To begin investing, you need to open an investment account (also known as a trading account). But even before doing that, you need to know a few things. This chapter discusses the first thing you need to be aware of.

If you go to a bank or a discount brokerage, you should be asked this question at first: *Would it be a registered or non-registered account?* The alternative phrasing of *an open or a registered account* might be used.

Let's discuss both open and registered accounts. It's up to you which type to start with. You can have either a registered account, or an open account, or both. The important part is to start.

I have both types of accounts, and after reading this chapter and this book, you will be able to figure out what type of account best suits you.

Open or Non-Registered Account

Non-registered accounts are not registered with the Canada Revenue Agency. This account type is more common than registered accounts. Now let's look at the advantages and disadvantages of both account types.

Advantages of an Open Account

- Easy to open—less paperwork.
- No limit on the amount of money you can deposit.
- No restrictions on withdrawing money.
- Amounts you withdraw are not taxed.
- You can keep this type of account as long as you live.

Disadvantages of an Open Account

- You don't get a tax break on your deposits.
- If it generates income, you pay taxes on your income.
- If you sell your holdings and achieve profit (capital gains), you pay taxes on the profit as well.

Registered Account

An RRSP (registered retirement savings plan), or registered account, is not something you actually buy. This is just an account type, and you buy qualified investments to hold inside that registered plan. Think of the RRSP as an umbrella sheltering you from the sun. Think of the sun as the Canada Revenue

Agency. As long as you are under the umbrella, you are protected from the heat. As long as you are inside your registered plan, you are protected from taxes.

Advantages of a Registered Account

- Deposits generate tax receipts to provide tax breaks.
- If the account generates income, no taxes have to be paid, because income is sheltered.
- If you sell your holdings and achieve profits, you pay no taxes on capital gains, but you pay withholding taxes on withdrawals.
- You pay no taxes on growth and switches made inside your account, as long as you are not going outside the registered plan.

Disadvantages of a Registered Account

- The account is registered with Canada revenue Agency (CRA). That's where the term *registered* comes from.
- You are only allowed to deposit so much money.
- Withdrawals are restricted.
- You are taxed on the amount you withdraw. The more money you withdraw, the more taxes you pay. See withholding tax rates listed at the end of this chapter.
- You can't keep this account forever. The account has to be terminated once you are 71, and you have to convert this account to a Registered Income Fund (RIF), from which you

have to receive annual income by law. Also, you can take out all your money once you are 71, but this is not a good idea, as you have to pay hefty taxes.

RRSP Annual Limit

You can only invest so much money into your RRSP. The formula goes as follows:

A + B − C, where

A = Any unused portion of prior year's contribution
B = 18% of prior year's earned income (up to a maximum for that tax year as below)
C = Pension adjustment for the current year (RPP contributions, etc.)

Contribution Limit

2006	$18,000
2007	$19,000
2008	$20, 000
2009	$21, 000
2010	$22, 000
2011	indexed*

*Starting in 2011, the limits will be indexed for inflation.

Miscellaneous

- Income can be earned in many forms. When your savings accounts pay interest, that is income. When your mutual funds pay distributions, that is income. When your stocks pay you more stocks, that is income.

- The amount you save by putting money in an RRSP depends on your marginal tax rate. The minimum tax savings will be 22% of your contribution—e.g., a $5,000 contribution would save you $5,000 × 22% = $1,100. But the same $5,000 would save you

  $1,400, if your marginal tax rate is 28%
  $2,150, if your marginal tax rate is 43%
  $2,500, if your marginal tax rate is 50%

- The amount of withholding taxes you pay by taking out money from an RRSP depends on the amount you are withdrawing. Follow the rate below:

  Default rates in Quebec

  $0–$5,000: 21%
  $5,000.01–$15,000: 26%
  $15,000.01 and up: 31%

  All other provinces

  $0–$5,000: 10%
  $5,000.01–$15,000: 20%
  $15,000.01 and up: 30%

- Although the registered account type looks very cool, many personal-finance columnists would argue that it is only tax deferred, not tax sheltered, because eventually, you pay taxes at a later date. There is no escape from paying taxes.

- If you are not sure what type of account to choose, just start with an open account for now. You will be able to change the account type later on.

Chapter 2

Why Keeping Money in a Bank Account Is Not Good Enough

You Are Not Alone

If you are reading this book, chances are high that you've never invested in your life, like many other Canadians. You are not alone; very few people actually invest. Just ask all your friends and family members, and see how many actively think, plan, and invest. We were never given any personal finance lessons in school and university, and we assume that we will be just fine in later years. Some of us are just happy to keep money in a savings account. We don't realize that if we don't plan and invest for the future, we will not be OK. Life expectancy is increasing every year, and we will run out of money before we even reach retirement. In this chapter, I will discuss why savings accounts are just not good enough. Even if your savings account offers a relatively high interest rate of 4%, you will lose money in the long run. Hard to believe? Keep on reading.

It's Called Inflation

Inflation will decrease the worth of your saved money over time. Inflation can be debated over nights and days, but to keep things simple, I will only discuss what you need to know.

The Effects of Inflation

You must have heard from complaints from older family members that a cup of coffee used to cost fifty cents or even less. These days, a cup of coffee is $1.25 to $2.00, or even more. This increase is a result of inflation. Inflation is defined as an increase in the price level for goods and services (basically everything). Inflation is measured by the Bank of Canada as an annual percentage increase. As inflation rises, your money buys less and less. A $100 bill today is not going to be the same as a $100 bill in 10 or 20 years. Coffee—and everything else—gradually becomes more expensive due to inflation.

The Flaw in Savings Accounts

Let's say your savings account is giving you 2% interest (in reality, big banks pay almost no interest). And consider that the annual inflation rate is 3%. If you keep $100 in your savings account for one year, you should have $102 in your hands after one year, right? Well, yes, technically, but that $102 is less than you started with. Due to inflation, you need $103 to buy same goods you would have bought with $100 a year ago. So actually, you lost money—$1, to be exact.

Losing just $1 does not feel that bad, but losing your chance at retirement funding will. The amount of money you could potentially lose is scary.

Inflation and Investments

There is no need to discuss the types and causes of inflation. But you need to know what you should do about inflation, and this should not be taken lightly. Investors should always adjust investment options and take necessary steps to minimize losses caused by inflation. If you keep all of your money in bank accounts, you will hit hard by inflation. Fixed-income investors—investors who invest in bonds, GICs, and savings accounts—are equally at risk.

If you invest in stocks, mutual funds, and the like, you should be OK in the long run; the important thing is to invest in the first place. This book emphasizes mutual funds for first-time investors. Mutual funds are made of stocks representing good companies. A good company's earnings should increase enough to keep up with or beat the pace of inflation.

Miscellaneous

- Stay away from savings accounts. Even if you hold one of those high interest–paying savings accounts, you will not beat inflation in the long run.

- Assume you invest $100 in a bond that pays 10% interest annually. After one year, you collect $110. What is your rate of return? 10%? It looks that way until you consider inflation. If the inflation rate is 5%, your actual rate of return is 5%, not 10%.

Chapter 3

You Don't Have to Be a Financial Guru to Start Investing

Investments Simplified

The purpose of this book is to broaden your knowledge and give you enough information to start investing on your own. You don't need an advisor, and you don't have to be rich to start investing. You don't need to listen to all those analysts' recommendations, and you don't need to subscribe to the *Wall Street Journal* or *Investors Daily*. You don't need to spend hours reading financial Web sites. All you need is little information—and, of course, the willingness to take action.

Let me tell you something that may sound ridiculous. But it is the truth, and it will never change. Here it is: *No one can predict the markets.* Not convinced? Predicting the markets is like predicting which numbers will win the lottery; no one ever has, and no one ever will. Don't be intimidated by all those analysts, economists, gurus and journalists. After reading this book and giving it your own perspective, you can be a cutting-edge investor. Just use the tools and knowledge mentioned here and start investing.

The funny thing about money is that everyone can give you advice about your money, but they are not nearly so casual with their own finances. No one cares about your money but you. You are one who earned it, and only you know the value of each dollar. Why give your money to someone else to invest? When you are your own money manager, you will try your best to serve your own interests while minimizing risk. You will never do frequent trading to earn commissions, and you will never make impulsive decisions. Self-interest is the best interest, which is why I don't believe you have to hire a financial advisor to start investing.

But before doing so, you need to know a little bit about financial markets and financial products. No worries here—I am not giving you an MBA course. Just read the next few pages, then give yourself a break if you need to absorb some of the material.

First, I will briefly mention world's major financial markets. You need to know this, even if you are not planning to invest. Every single person living in this century should know the basics of financial markets and financial products. These basics will help you to gain a better understanding of financial information and will empower you to make better, informed financial decisions. These basics are the same regardless of where you live, who you are, and what you do.

Chapter 4

Financial Markets

What Are Financial Markets?

If you keep your eyes open, it's almost impossible to end any given day without noticing anything related to financial markets. Yes, I am talking about the stock markets. A stock market is just like any other market you know, such as the fish market, farmer's market and so on. The only difference is, in the stock market, people are buying and selling stocks (or other types of financial instruments, such as bonds, options, commodities and so on). The term "stock market" is so general that it can mean any of hundreds or thousands of financial trading places.

 No one knows for sure where or how the idea of stock market was born. Many believe that Italians started it in the later 11th century; many others believe that in Egypt in the early 11th century, Jews and Islamic merchants set up the earliest form of market that dealt with credit and payment. Here in North America, the New York Stock Exchange is the oldest (established in 1792) and the largest.

Physical and Electronic Markets

"Stock market" can refer to financial instruments trading through various ways. Financial instruments can be bought in actual, physical places or electronically, through electronic markets. These financial markets, either electronic or physical, can be called stock exchanges. A stock exchange is a place where buyers and sellers can communicate and transact with each other. Buyers can be investors, like you, or a mutual-fund company or foreign government. Basically, anyone can be a buyer. Likewise, anyone can be a seller.

The purpose of a stock exchange is to match buyers with sellers. Let's say you are willing to buy 1,000 shares of XYZ Company. In order to do so, you have to place your buy order through an advisor, a discount brokerage or a securities dealer. These people are licensed to buy or sell stocks or securities once on your behalf. Once your order is in place, your advisor or broker has to find a seller who is willing to sell what you are willing to buy. Once the buyer and seller agree with each other on price, amount, and so on, the transaction takes place.

Your XYZ Company may be listed or traded on a physical exchange, like the Toronto Stock Exchange, or traded on an electronic exchange, like NASDAQ. I will explain these exchanges more a little later.

Let me clarify something right here. A lot of us think that when we are buying shares, we are buying them directly from the company. This is not true. You are buying not from the company but from someone who owns stock in that company and is selling. We can only buy shares from a company directly when a privately held company decides to go public. These shares are called IPO (initial public offering). A company issues

IPO to raise money when it goes public for the first time. (Also, from time to time, a company may issue new shares to the public when it needs money, but this isn't a common practice.) Even when you buy from a company in an IPO, you still make that purchase through an agent.

How We Measure Stock Exchange

An exchange or index can use either the price-weighted method or the market value/capitalization method to measure prices. In a price-weighted method, the price of each stock or company is used, and each stock is a part of the index in proportion to its price. According to that method, a little price change of a single stock can change the value of the exchange greatly, regardless of the size of the company. The market value/capitalization method is the opposite. In this method, each stock is a part of the index in proportion to its market value. A small change in the price of a big company can change the value of the exchange greatly.

World's Largest Exchanges

Here are the world's largest exchanges as of 2006 by market capitalization.

- New York Stock Exchange
- Tokyo Stock Exchange
- NASDAQ
- London Stock Exchange

- Euro Next
- Toronto Stock Exchange
- Frankfurt Stock Exchange
- Hong Kong Stock Exchange
- Milan Stock Exchange
- Madrid Stock Exchange

Exchanges You Need To Know

Very briefly, I will describe three major exchanges you need to be familiar with. I am not describing all ten exchanges, because I will explain the world's important indices (not exchanges) later on, and that should acquaint you with all the exchanges. Indices were created to measure exchanges or stocks (trading on one or more exchanges) more meaningfully.

Toronto Stock Exchange: The largest in Canada, third largest in North America, and sixth largest in the world. The Toronto Stock Exchange trades only equities. In 2002, the exchange adopted TSX branding and since been called S&P/TSX. In the past, the Toronto Stock Exchange used to be called TSE, but currently "TSE" denotes the Tokyo Stock Exchange.

New York Stock Exchange (NYSE): The largest and oldest exchange in the United States. Still today, trading is done on the trading floor, face-to-face and physically. Only listed stocks can be traded in the physical exchange.

NASDAQ: The National Association of Securities Dealers Automated Quotations, or NASDAQ, started in 1972 as a virtual exchange. Computers or electronic systems match buyers and sellers, and that's how trading is done. NASDAQ has been called the index of the new economy.

That's enough about exchanges. Now we will discuss the world's major indices. After reading this chapter, you should have a good idea of the world's exchanges and indices. Obviously, I am merely providing a summary of how these systems work, but you don't need more than a basic understanding as a first-time investor. At the end of this book, I will direct you to a list of Web sites and magazines that offer further information. Keeping yourself updated with latest investment news is very important, and I will show you how to do so.

Stock Market Index

The term "index" is deeply associated with the stock market. Whenever you hear people talking about the market, most likely they are talking about an index. But what is an index?

An index is a group of stocks; the statistical changes of the member stocks are measured as a whole. Indices were created to make life a little bit simpler. So many stocks are trading on different exchanges in different countries—it is surely impossible to track all these stocks. Also, stocks often belong very specifically to one industry, such as biotechnology, telecommunications, health sciences and so on. If you want to track the financial news of an industry, imagine how many stocks you would have to monitor at once. That's why indices were created. Indices can track the activity within a certain country, sector, exchange, region and so on. Many indices can exist in the same exchange, same country, or same industry, tracking different sets of stocks.

Major World Indices You Need to Know

If you tried to follow every index in existence, you would go insane. As a first-time Canadian investor, you need to know only a few of them; following two to four indices will suffice. Let me describe now only those you need to know. I will not discuss how to calculate indices yet, because I don't think that's necessary at this stage. But remember, there are mainly two ways to measure indices: the price-weighted method and market value/capitalization weighted method.

S&P/TSX Composite Index: S&P/TSX Composite Index is a market value/capitalization weighted index. This index is considered the benchmark for Canadian equities and is also viewed as an indicator for the health of the Canadian economy. Also, pension-fund and mutual-fund managers use this index as benchmark to compare rates of returns. Roughly 71% of this index is composed of Canadian-based companies listed on the Toronto Stock Exchange. In the past, S&P/TSX used to be called TSE 300 Composite Index, or just TSE 300. TSE 300 started in 1977, but it was developed in 1975 with a base level of 1000. (The base level is the lowest index level, or a starting index level, of a stock exchange.) TSE 300 was made of 300 companies, although it varied from year to year. Companies were added or dropped based on exchange criteria. New York's Standard and Poor Corporation took over the management of TSE 300 on May 1, 2002, and the name S&P/TSX came into effect. Now S&P/TSX has no fixed number of companies and has imposed higher standards for companies to be added.

Dow Jones Industrial Average: The world's most recognized index —often simply referred to as "the market." When using that phrase, the media and investors are usually referring to the DJIA. Charles H. Dow started the DJIA in 1896 with only 12 companies. Today, the Dow consists of the 30 largest and best-known companies in the United States. The DJIA is looked after by the editors of the *Wall Street Journal.* The DJIA is a price-weighted index. When started in 1896, the DJIA was calculated according to the average price of those original 12 stocks. World-famous and reputable companies like Coca-Cola, Boeing, Exxon, IBM, McDonalds, Microsoft and Wal-Mart are members of the DJIA. Everyone knows about these companies, which are unlikely to disappear overnight.

The Standard and Poor's 500: The Standard and Poor's 500 (or S&P 500) index represents large-cap companies and is considered one of the best benchmarks for both the U.S. stock market and the world at large. It covers all major market sectors and all areas of the U.S. economy. The S&P 500 accounts for 70% of the U.S. market.

The NASDAQ Composite: The NASDAQ composite index is made of all companies that trade on the NASDAQ exchange. Its eight subindices are telecommunications, transportation, biotechnology, computers, industrials, banking, insurance and finance. The NASDAQ is a market value/capitalization weighted index and heavily weighted in technology and internet stocks. The NASDAQ is considered very volatile and speculative, but companies listed here also have high growth potential. The NASDAQ, which includes 500 to 600 companies, has been called the index of the new economy.

Other indices: I have covered major North American indices. Now I will just mention a few other indices. You only need to know which country each represents. If you watch the news, you will come across these names and be able to recognize represented countries.

FTSE100	Britain
DAX	Germany
CAC40	France
NIKKEI	Japan
HANG SENG	Hong Kong

Miscellaneous

- The two major ways to measure stock exchanges or indices are the price-weighted method and market value/capitalization weighted method.

- In the price-weighted method, each stock is a part of the index in proportion to its price.

- In the market value/capitalization method, each stock is a part of the index in proportion to its market value.

- The plural of index is "indices." "Indexes" also can be used as the plural, but this is less common.

- This flow chart might help you to look at the whole picture at a glance:

  Financial Markets → Stock markets → Stock Exchanges → Stock Indices

Chapter 5

Financial Products

What Are Financial Products?

Financial products can be commonly known, such as stocks, bonds and mutual funds, or can be more obscure, such as ADR, flow-through investments, naked call, married put and so on. The world of financial products is endless. A million-dollar trade—or higher—is being made every second throughout the world. The amounts being traded in our interconnected global markets are simply unimaginable. Roughly $400 trillion, or $400,000,000,000,000, is traded yearly in the currency markets worldwide—$20 trillion in stocks, $30 trillion in bonds and so on. While you and I are wrapping up our North American markets, traders on the other side of the world are just starting of their day.

Financial products can be very simple or very complex, and one main product can lead to many other products. Millions of books, jobs, analysts and financial companies deal with one or more of these products. One transaction leads to another and another, in an endless cycle.

As a first-time investor or even as a veteran investor, you don't need to master all these products. But you do need to know the most basic and important ones, and this chapter will teach you just that. We will start with the most famous and well-known one—yes, stocks.

Stocks

A stock is an investment product issued by a corporation that grants partial ownership of the assets and earnings of the corporation. Simply stated, a stockholder is an owner of the corporation. Let's say a company issued 100 stocks, and you bought 1 stock. Technically, you are an owner of this company, but your cut is 1/100th of the company. The more stocks you buy, the larger percentage of ownership you will have.

I can't resist telling one personal story here. If you ride the Toronto Transit Authority, or TTC, you will notice most of their trains are manufactured by Bombardier. Bombardier is a well-known Canadian train and plane manufacturer—probably the second-or third-largest manufacturer in the world. I hold some Bombardier shares. Once, I was on the subway with my friends, and I told them I am one of the owners of this train manufacturer. I wish you could have seen their faces. They were looking at me as if I were a multi-millionaire. My friends did not know that you only need one share to claim ownership. Such privilege is the beauty of a capitalist society, and I love it.

The word "stock" is interchangeable with "share," "equity," "security" and so on. There are two types of stock you need to know: common stock and preferred stock.

Common Stock: "Stock" most often refers to common stock. Common stock holders have voting rights at shareholders' meetings or in decisions. Also, common share holders receive dividends or earnings. If you are a common share holder, you are directly involved in the failure or success of the company. If the company goes bankrupt, you have a good chance of losing all your investments.

Preferred Share: Preferred share owners also have some degree of ownership, but this version offers limited reward with reduced risks. These owners have no voting rights. In case of bankruptcy, preferred share owners have priority over common stock, which means they might get some of their money back if the company goes bankrupt. Dividends paid on these stocks are fixed and guaranteed.

Bonds

The bond is the second most popular financial instrument after stock. A bond is an investment product that is very different from stocks. A bond is a debt instrument that entitles the company (or government) to borrow money from the investor. In return, the investor collects interest for a specific period of time and gets his money (principal) back at the end of the term. Buying a bond is nothing but lending money to a company or government.

Bond is debt investment, and stock is equity investment. When you buy bonds, you are lending money to the issuer, and you have higher claims on the company's assets if it goes bankrupt. On the other hand, when you buy stocks, you share ownership and profits.

Let's go over some terms that you need to know. You probably have heard these terms before.

Market value: The price at which bonds are being bought or sold.

Face value or *par value:* This is the amount at maturity, or the borrowed amount you will get back.

Interest rates/coupon: Simply the interest a bond pays until maturity. In the old days, each interest payment was represented by a coupon, and the investor had to tear off the coupon to collect interest. These days, all payments are electronic—no more cutting coupons.

Yield: To calculate yield, divide the coupon amount by the price. Yield is the actual amount of interest you earn in percentage. When you buy a bond at par, yield equals the interest rate. When you buy a bond in the secondary market (after issue date), yield may not equal the interest rate. Yield changes with the price.

Yield to maturity: Just as the name says, this figure tells you the total return if you hold a bond until maturity. Don't worry too much about this figure. The formula to calculate YTM is more complicated than simple yield.

Types of Bonds

Let's discuss major bond types you need to know. You will come across these once in a while.

Corporate Bonds: Corporations issue these bonds to borrow money. The term can be from 1 to 100 years. Corporate bonds provide higher yield due to higher risks.

The following are very common corporate bonds.

Debentures: Corporate bonds backed by the general credit of the corporation. Debentures are very common.

Asset-backed bonds: Backed by corporate assets, such as equipment or properties.

Convertible bonds: Can be converted into stocks.

Callable bonds: Company can call (redeem) these before maturity.

Government bonds: Backed by governments. Government bonds issued by rich countries are more liquid than government bonds issued by poor countries—that is, you can more easily cash bonds from rich countries because they have the money immediately ready to pay the value of the bond Treasury notes and treasury bills are world-famous in this category.

*Treasury note*s: T-notes are globally popular and very easy to buy and sell from the U.S. government or through banks. These bonds pay fixed interest and mature in 1 to 10 years. Interest payments are made every six months.

Treasury bills: T-Bills are short-term government debt with no interest. You buy this at a discount, and your gain is the difference between the discount price and par value.

Municipal bonds: Issued by local or municipal governments.

The following two are very common municipal bonds.

General-obligation bond: Backed by the credit reputation or faith of the issuer.

Revenue bonds: Backed by the revenue or income of the issuer. Can be tied to a new project or task, such as a new mall or a new highway.

Zero-coupon bond: The name explains it all: this bond has zero coupons, meaning it pays no interest. You buy these at a deeply discounted price (lower than par value) and sell (when mature) at par value. The difference is your profit. Any type of bond can be a zero-coupon bonds; governments or corporations or municipalities can issue zero-coupon bonds.

The following time chart shows the maturity time frames for different types of bonds.

Time Chart

Corporate bonds:	1–100 years
Municipal bonds:	1–50 years
T–notes:	1–10 years
T-bills:	Less than 1 year

GIC

The guaranteed investment certificate, or GIC, is a modified version of a savings account. You get a guaranteed rate of return, just like with a savings account, but you have to hold your money for a specific period of time. A GIC's lifespan can range from 1 to 5 years. This is very inconvenient, which is why this certificate pays higher interest than a bank account. Banks or trust companies manufacture GICs, and they are very easy to buy and sell.

These days, financial institutions have come up with various versions of the GIC. The following are modified GICs.

Index-linked or *market-linked GICs* track indices or markets with a guarantee of capital preservation.

A *cashable GIC* is one that you can cash before it reaches maturity.

An *escalating-rate GIC* adjusts its interest rate with current interest rates.

Regardless of what the manufacturers tell you, GICs offer lean rewards, if any, and you should always stay away from them. GICs are not free; there are fees attached. If you are thinking of investing in GICs, a high-interest savings account might be a better option. Explore all your other options first before jumping into GICs. Young people should not be in GICs.

If you can't accept a little market volatility and would like to be super-safe, a savings account is a better option than a GIC.

Chapter 6

Mutual Funds: The First-Time Investor's Friend

What Are Mutual Funds?

If you had a friend who was very knowledgeable in the stock market, you would definitely want him to manage your stock investments. What if this friend agreed to do everything for a small fee? Wouldn't you hire him? A mutual fund is just like this hypothetical friend. A mutual fund is a collection of investment products, such as stocks, bonds, T-bills, and so on. Mutual fund companies collect money from investors and hire professionals to manage your money. These professionals are called fund managers. When you buy a mutual fund, you buy a portion of the fund (or a portion of what the funds hold altogether).

Why Are Mutual Funds Suitable for First-Time Investors?

You need years of experience, lots of money, intensive knowledge, and various tools to pick an individual stock. A mutual fund does all that for you while keeping risk to a minimum. It's no wonder that mutual funds' assets are skyrocketing with the speed of a space shuttle.

To pick the most suitable funds for you, you need to know a few things. Let me start with the advantages of mutual funds; you can use these advantages to overcome obstacles you will face as a first-time investor.

Chapter 7

Advantages of Mutual Funds

Low Minimums and PAC

Low minimums are the best feature mutual funds offer. Have you heard your friends saying they don't have enough money to invest, and that's why they never save? If you are using same excuse, put it aside. Most mutual funds will let you start with as little as $500, and some will let you start with just $100. If you agree to let fund companies take money out of your bank account systematically—either monthly, weekly, biweekly, quarterly, semi-annually or annually, you can start with as little as $25. This convenient option is a good one for those who can't put in one lump-sum payment to start with. You will not find this type of convenience investing in stocks and bonds. The above-mentioned feature is called PAC (pre-authorized checking), AIP (automatic investment plan) or SIP (systematic investment plan). I will use PAC in this book, because PAC is widely used and recognized.

PAC is nothing but systematically investing your money with a financial institution. One great advantage of having PAC is that it gives you the power of dollar-cost averaging.

Dollar-cost average simply refers to the averaging of your cost per share or per unit. Suppose you are running a PAC for $25 monthly on the 15th of each month. Your mutual fund unit price will not be the same on the 15th of each month. But you will be adding the same $25 each month. If unit price goes up, you will be buying fewer units. If unit price goes down, you will be buying more units. Running a PAC year after year and calculating your average cost per share after a few years will prompt gains. Research has shown that if you do dollar-cost averaging, you end up buying more units rather than spending one set lump sum.

Dollar-cost averaging on stocks or bonds will cost you a lot of money, with transaction fees every time you buy. But you can do a dollar-cost average on mutual funds without additional cost or transaction fees. Just run a PAC, and you are good to go. This feature is very suitable for first-time investors.

Professional Management

Choosing an individual stock or bond can be an enormous task for new investors. All the research and decision-making can be daunting. Everyday investors don't have the tools or resources to make a prudent decision. When you buy mutual funds, you are buying the expertise and service of the group of professionals who manage those funds. Each group consists of a fund manager and a few analysts. This group is responsible for doing all the research and for deciding when and what to buy and sell. Basically, everything is done by the fund manager and his team.

You don't have to spend days and nights analyzing stocks and monitoring your portfolio. Remember, these professionals cost you money, but I will discuss how to keep your costs minimal.

Diversification and Convenience

Whether you are a stock or a mutual-fund investor, it is very important to diversify. The old saying "Don't put all your eggs in one basket" still applies. Diversification reduces your risk by spreading your money across different companies, countries and types of assets. A mutual fund is lot more diversified than a stock or a bond, because a typical fund holds 20 to 50 stocks or a mixture of stocks, bonds, T-bills and so on. I will share my own simple diversification strategy a little later.

Diversification can be a headache if you invest in stocks or bonds. You need to do lots of trading, and you have to keep track all of your portfolios constantly. If you don't mind the complex task of managing your own portfolio and enjoy doing it, that's fine. But such an endeavour would require a lot of effort for first-time investors as they pick different types of investment products and attempt to manage them. A mutual fund gives you exposure throughout the world with diversification and convenience—nothing needed from your side.

Regulation

When I first started investing, a junior mining company's stock was going through the roof. This ten-cent stock was trading at close to two dollars, and rumour was it would reach five dollars soon. I started dreaming of becoming a millionaire in couple of weeks and had already made some plans to retire in the Bahamas the next month.

My emotions ran high; I did not hesitate to invest a few thousand dollars. My investment went up for one day. Starting the second day, my investment started to fall, and after one week my investment was down to four hundred dollars. Basically, I lost all my money. In a mutual fund, it is unlikely that you will lose your money overnight. In the financial world, nothing is guaranteed, but a mutual fund offers a better degree of protection than stocks due to stringent rules and regulations. Mutual funds are highly regulated, ensuring how funds are managed and how investors are informed.

A few points on mutual funds are worth mentioning.

A mutual-fund company does not physically hold its assets. A third party, called the custodian, holds securities on behalf of the fund company. If the fund company is in trouble, your money is protected. Fund managers can't just walk out with your money. The custodian can be either a bank or a trust company.

Fund companies need approval from unit holders to make any significant change. Also, any change in the fund's investment objective has to be approved by unit holders.

Fund companies have to disclose the fund's holdings on a regular basis.

Fund companies have to disclose the fund's unit value regularly.

Fund companies need to publish procedures for the purchase and sale of funds.

Remember, these rules are in place to provide you some degree of safety. No investment is guaranteed, and any investment can decline in value.

Liquidity

Mutual funds are very easy to sell and buy. Your money is not tied up for any specified terms or years. Keep in mind that, except for money-market funds, you will incur an early redemption fee if you redeem your fund within the first sixty days of purchase. Consult your mutual-fund prospectus to find out more.

Transaction Cost

Mutual funds offer another convenient feature. Suppose you want to buy a few Canadian stocks and a couple of international stocks to start your investment. You will be spending the following if you are buying stocks:

(Assume trading cost per transaction is $29)
Three Canadian stocks trading on TSX = 3 × $29 = $87 CAD
Two American stocks trading on NYSE = 2 × $29 = $58 US

Imagine your cost in buying on the European and Asian exchanges. Selling would be equally expensive. You can avoid all these costs if you buy mutual funds. However, you do pay on mutual funds, and I will explain how in a moment.

Chapter 8

Disadvantages of Mutual Funds

Nothing in life comes without disadvantages. Now that we have discussed the pros of mutual funds, let's go over the cons.

Fees and Expenses

When you buy mutual funds, you pay fees to compensate companies for doing all the work. These fees are called management-expense ratios (MERs). Depending on what type of load (front load, back load or low load) you buy, you might pay commission and redemption fees. I will discuss MERs and load a little later in order to show you how to keep your cost minimal.

No Insurance

The Canadian Deposit Insurance Corporation (CDIC) does not insure mutual funds the way it insures bank accounts, loans and so on. Keep in mind that other investments, such as stocks or bonds, are not insured by the CDIC either.

Loss of Controls

Fund managers, not mutual fund holders, make the decisions on a fund's portfolio. When you buy mutual funds, you give up your authority and abide by the fund company's decisions.

Trading Limitations

Stocks can be traded as many times as you want throughout the day (North American markets are open from 9:30 a.m. to 4:00 p.m., Monday through Friday). Mutual funds are priced only once a day, after the markets close. Regardless of how many times you buy or sell in a day, you will get only one price for that day. It does not change every second, like stocks.

Cash Holding

Mutual funds need to hold large amounts of cash to pay for redemptions (when someone is selling). Had this cash been invested, you would have made money on this cash. In other words, investors lose growth potential on that cash portion.

Mutual funds carry some other disadvantages, but these are the most important ones.

Next, let's discuss the fees and expenses you pay when you buy mutual funds. Fees and expenses are very important to know, as such information allows you to cut costs by investing carefully. You need to do that to become a successful investor.

Chapter 9

Fees and Expenses

What Are Fees and Expenses?

Mutual funds would be an unbeatable investment vehicle if there were no fees. But without charging fees, fund companies would not be able to give you all these options. Many financial gurus and critics would tell you to avoid mutual funds because of these fees and expenses, but I beg to differ. I think it's better to pay fees than to lose all your money. When you buy stocks, you pay to do that—and then pay again to sell. In mutual funds, things are different. You pay your fund company every day for as long as you hold the fund. So if you calculate the cost of a thousand dollars' worth of investments in both stocks and mutual funds for ten years, your cost for mutual funds will definitely be higher.

Let's look at these examples:

$1000 in mutual funds:
A 3% MER would cost $1000 × 3%, which equals $30 a year.
The 10-year cost is $30 × 10, which equals $300.

$1000 in stocks:

Standard trading fees to buy = $29
Standard trading fees to sell = $29
Total cost in 10 years = $58

Buying stocks looks good in the above example—*if* your stocks make money. Compared to losing your money in stocks, you would not mind paying fees to buy mutual funds instead. I invest in both mutual funds and stocks. In last 10+ years, a couple of my stocks have evaporated almost overnight. I lost money in mutual funds too, but the margins were very slim. I have never lost my whole investment in mutual funds. If you know any investors, ask them how many times they lost money in stocks and how many times they lost money in mutual funds. You will get the obvious answers. Try it!

Beware of and Avoid Mutual Fund Fees and Expenses

It is time to explain the fees and expenses associated with mutual funds. An educated investor, who knows how these costs and expenses occur, should be able to reduce overall costs significantly, thus achieving higher return.

MER

This is the major cost of holding a mutual fund. MER stands for management expense ratio. The MER measures a fund's total expenses for a financial year. A MER calculates a fund's expenses by the fund's average assets. The MER is expressed as a percentage of the fund's total net assets. If you break down the MER, you will get

$$MER = (M + ER) \times GST$$

The M stands for "management fees." The M is the big chunk of the MER. This is where fund companies make money. Management fees cover compensations to dealers, sales and marketing costs, corporate expenses, portfolio-management cost, investment research cost and so on.

The ER stands for "expense ratio." Expense ratios include administrative costs, such as regulatory costs (provincial and federal), client services and administrative costs, custodian fees, fund-reporting costs (annual report, prospectus and so on), audit and legal costs, technology costs and so on.

GST: Yes, you pay tax again when you invest your already-taxed dollars.

The MER can be found in a fund's prospectus and on the Internet. Also, you can call your fund company to obtain the MER. It is important that your funds do not have a skyrocketing MER. Always pick a fund with a reasonable MER—not more than 2.5%. You can actually shop around for a certain type of fund and pick one with a lower MER. I will discuss index funds shortly, which have a low MER compared to regular mutual funds.

The MER Mystery

New investors will be puzzled when they do not see costs, mainly MERs, coming out of their investments up front. It's not on your statement, not on your receipts, not on your confirmation slips ... not anywhere. Does that mean that fund companies are not charging you MER fees? Are they giving you everything for free?

No, not at all. You see, fund companies came up with this brilliant way to charge you invisibly every day. The MER comes off a fund's NAV (or net asset value—the fund's price per unit) every day, so you don't see it. That's why it is important to hold a fund with a reasonable MER: in the long run, you don't want to evaporate your money by paying a high MER. Usually, Canadian funds have a lower MER than specialty funds (which we will discuss later), and specialty funds have a higher MER than foreign funds.

Huge MER gaps can exist. A Canadian equity fund at one fund company can have a 2% MER, and the same type of Canadian equity fund at another fund company can have a 3% MER. A higher MER does not necessarily mean a higher rate of return.

Let me give you a simple example of how you pay MERs invisibly. Suppose your fund's actual unit price is $10.05 for any given day before adding any expenses or MERs. Now your fund company will add their daily cost to $10.05 and will charge you $10.30 (assuming cost for one day is $0.25). You will never see the actual value $10.05 anywhere. Investors will see $10.30, and this is what the fund company will publish on their Web site or in the newspaper as the NAV for that day. I wish fund companies would disclose MERs visibly, but it does not look like that will happen any time soon. That's why you absolutely must do your homework before you invest anywhere.

Loads

Mutual funds come in a confusing variety of packages: front-end load, back-end load, low load, or even no-load. Let's clarify these.

Front-end load: When you buy this load, you pay your dealer's commission up front. Commissions can run from 0%

to 5%. If you are buying $1000 worth of funds with a 5% commission, your dealer is receiving $50, and only $950 is getting invested. With this option, you don't pay any charges or fees when you redeem your funds. Always buy front-end funds at 0% commission, so you invest the full amount. This option is also known as initial service charge, or ISC.

Back-end load: When you buy this load, you are agreeing to stick to your fund for a few years (usually seven), and if you withdraw before passing those years, you will get hit by redemption fees. Redemption fees decline every year until they no longer exist at all. If you have always wondered why your broker or dealer always wants you to hook up with back-end funds, it's because these funds give them a flat up-front commission (usually 5%) from the fund company. Who eventually pays this commission? It's you. Buying back-end means you have to stick to the fund for many years, or pay redemption fees, just to compensate your fund company for that commission. Your goal is to stay away from back-end load. Back-end load is also known as rear-end load, deferred sales charge (DSC) and so on.

Low-load: This one is a kind of back-end load with reduced commitment lengths (usually three years) and reduced redemption fees as well. Also stay away from this load.

No-load: This is just a 0% version of a front-end load. But make sure the MER is not higher than other loads, in which case this is a good option.

Trailer Fees

Fund companies pay your broker or dealer trailer fees as long as you hold the fund. Trailer fees are already in the MER. Trailer fees are service commission fees, meaning your dealer or broker should keep funds on track, answer your questions, service your accounts and so on. Generally, front-end funds pay 1%, and back-end funds pay 0.5% trailer fees.

Turnover Ratio

The turnover ratio tells you how actively your fund manager is trading. Lots of trading can be expensive. The higher the turnover ratio, the more expensive the fund is. For an open account, a high turnover ratio can translate into high tax bills. You should be able to find this information in your mutual-fund prospectus.

The Prospectus: Your Mutual-Fund Bible

I have described some of the fees and expenses involved with buying a mutual fund. There might be more fees and expenses, along with other risks. A successful investor is an educated investor who researches fees, expenses, and risks. Remember, an emotional decision will not make you a successful investor. Plenty of tools out there can help you with your research, and this book will show you those tools.

The prospectus is a powerful tool that will help you a lot with your research. A prospectus is a selling document published by fund companies. By law, this has to be distributed to you as an investor. This document, which looks like a magazine, must explain a fund's objectives, holdings, performance, risks, fees, expenses and so on. In plain words, it must provide full and true disclosure of all the important stuff you need to know to make an informed and educated decision. You can obtain this document by calling your fund company, or you can download a copy on your fund company's Web site for free.

Always read the prospectus carefully and thoroughly. Dissect all the information it provides and then reread key information, such as risks and costs.

Miscellaneous

- Pick funds with a reasonable MER. Be extra-cautious not to pick a fund with more than a 2.5% MER. The same types of funds can have different MERs at different fund companies. If my fund company charges me a higher MER for the same kind of fund, there had better be some explanations justifying that higher MER.

- The MER is shown annually and calculated daily. The NAV you are paying for each unit already includes the MER; you do not pay the MER separately.

- The NAV, or net asset value, is what you pay for your funds. In mutual funds, you buy one unit or one share, just like one stock or one bond. The NAV equals the fund's assets minus the fund's liabilities. Fund companies price their funds every business day after markets close. The NAV is what you see in the newspaper or on Web sites in the Fund Prices section.

- Fund companies pay your broker, dealer, or discount brokerage trailer fees as long as you hold your funds.

The Trailer Chart

Load Type	Fund Companies Pay
Front-load	Up to 1% annually
Back-load	Up to 0.5% annually
Low-load	Pays same as back-load at first, but later changes to front-load

- At www.sedar.com, you can find documents submitted by public companies and mutual-fund companies. You will be able to access mutual fund prospectuses, annual reports, financial statements and so on. This is a good place to start your research. Check this site whenever you need to look for a document and you don't want to wait for the paper version to arrive in the mail.

Chapter 10

Types of Funds

Open-End and Closed-End Funds

Before I describe the different types of funds, you need to know about open-end and closed-end funds. Most of the funds investors deal with are open-end funds. Open-end funds have unlimited units to sell and buy, as long as the fund manager is not closing or capping the fund. Closed-end funds have fixed numbers of units and trade on a stock exchange, just like stocks. An example would be the DDJ High Yield Fund, which trades on the Toronto Stock Exchange under HYB.UN.

These days, mutual funds are a hot commodity. Roughly 11,000 funds are available in North America. In other words, funds outnumber stocks.

In the basic level, there are three types of funds.

1. Equity funds
2. Income funds
3. Money-market funds

Your portfolio must include both equity funds and income funds. Shortly, I will show you my model portfolio to help you build your own. I will not include any money-market funds in my model portfolios, as money-market funds are just like interest-paying savings accounts. First-time investors should not be investing just to collect interest.

If you would like to follow a more conservative approach, you can add 5%–10% money-market funds into your portfolio.

Now, let me explain these three types. We will start with equity funds.

Equity Funds

As the name says, equity funds are made of equities, or stocks. Just as there are different types of equities, there are different types of equity funds. Fund managers can choose value or growth styles to manage equity funds (these styles are varied along a spectrum, but I will stick to the basics). Growth-fund managers pick the fastest-growing and often well-known companies to earn an above-average return. Growth managers will not care about stock price; they are willing to pay higher prices. Growth funds tend to be volatile. Value managers are looking for value or stocks that are trading at lower than their real value. Value funds are conservative funds that typically carry less risk than growth funds. Value managers hope to make profit from capital appreciation (meaning the profit will be made by selling stocks when they go higher).

Income Funds

Income funds are also known as fixed-income funds or bond funds. These funds are designed to give you a steady stream of income to diversify your portfolio. Income funds are supposed to give you more income than savings accounts or GICs. Like any investment, income funds are not risk-free. Senior and conservative investors tend to like income funds more than other investors.

Money-Market Funds

Money-market funds are like savings accounts that pay high interest. The unit value does not fluctuate, and the fund pays a monthly dividend or interest. Money-market funds should only be used to park money for a few days.

Some Other Types

Let's briefly examine the following types of funds, just to give you an idea.

Ethical funds: These funds will not invest in companies that deal with alcohol, tobacco, weapons, environmental pollution, the injuring of animals and so on. In Canada, not many fund companies offer ethical funds.

Sector funds: These are industry-specific funds—such as telecommunications, health science, biotechnology and so on. These funds can give you higher rate of return if your sector does well, but also can take a nose-dive if your sector tanks.

Regional funds: These funds are concentrated in specific regions, like the Pacific region, an emerging-market region, the Eastern European region, the Asian region and so on. Like sector funds, these funds can be risky and have higher MERs.

Segregated funds: This chapter would be incomplete without a discussion of these funds. A segregated fund is a mutual fund with an insurance wrapper; you can call it a hybrid fund. This type of fund offers the growth potential of a mutual fund plus some insurance protection features. Usually insurance protection guarantees your capital up to 100% at death and at maturity. To benefit, you have to either die or stick to your funds for ten or more years. This confuses investors. If you redeem your funds before ten years, there are no guarantees, and if markets perform badly, you will be losing your money in addition to paying a high MER. Segregated funds offer many other added features, but I will not discuss those, as there is no point in paying a high MER for features that won't exist for a decade. In the long run, holding segregated funds can cost you hefty fees, dragging down the rate of return. If you are that sensitive about money and need insurance features to protect your money, maybe you should avoid investing altogether. Let me give you an example of how MERs can vary between the two same funds.

CI Global Fund:	2.36% MER
CI Global GIF Class A Fund:	4.68% MER

(MER Source: CI's Web site at www.ci.com)

Specialty funds: Many fancy funds exist: hedge funds, labour-sponsored funds, institutional managed funds, fee-based wrap funds, and so many more. Remember one thing: these fancy funds charge you fancy fees ... and at the end, they empty your pockets. Stick to simple funds with low MERs or to plain index funds. I really like index funds and have dedicated an entire chapter to them.

Miscellaneous

- "Portfolio" refers to the main account under which you hold all your investment products. If you hold stocks, bonds, and mutual funds in one place, you can say you hold these in your portfolio.

- An annual report is different from a prospectus. You will find your fund's holdings (all of them, including stocks, bonds, T-bills and so on) and financial statements in an annual report. The annual report gives you some other important information as well. It's a good idea to check both the annual report and the prospectus.

- Young and aggressive investors tend to like equity funds more than other investors.

- Mutual funds can be categorized by the market capitalization of the stocks. Small-cap funds hold small-cap stocks. Small-cap companies have a market capitalization of less than 500 million dollars. Mid-cap funds hold mid-cap stocks. Mid-cap companies have a market-capitalization of 500 million to 5 billion dollars. Large-cap funds hold large-cap stock. Large-cap companies have a market capitalization of over 5 billion dollars.

- Balanced funds are just a blend of equity and income funds (typically 60% equity and 40% income). These funds are supposed to balance capital appreciation, income and safety.

- A global fund invests throughout the world, including in your own country. An international fund invests internationally, excluding your own country. In Canada, global funds hold a good portion of U.S. stocks, but international funds do not.

- The term "segregated" refers to the insurance companies' need to keep segregated-funds assets separated from their other products' assets.

Chapter 11

The Easy Portfolio

How Should I Build My Portfolio?

The old saying "Don't put all your eggs in one basket" was good advice 100 years ago, and it will be good advice forever. Whether you are a first-time or a veteran investor, you always need to spread out your investments to minimize your risks. You can diversify your investments by buying many funds from different fund companies or from the same fund company. Fund companies also offer what is known as a fund of funds—basically one fund holding five to fifteen other funds to give you broad diversification. An example would be CI Portfolio Series Funds. One main disadvantage of these funds is that you rely on the allocations of fund companies. Fund companies put in 10% of this fund and 20% of that fund in order to build a fund of funds, and you have no choice but to take whatever the fund companies are fixing for you. Also, the funds they are fixing for you obviously are their own funds. If you are buying this type of fund, avoid high MERs.

Easy and Simple

My idea of diversification is keep everything easy and simple. Holding too many funds can involve a lot of maintenance—you have to deal with many statements, tax receipts, records and so on. Let me introduce to you my own idea of keeping things simple. I will call it "the easy portfolio." The easy portfolio is made of four different types of mutual funds:

Canadian equity = 25%
Canadian income = 25%
Non-Canadian equity = 25%
Non-Canadian income = 25%

The Canadian-equity portion gives you capital appreciation from great Canadian companies.

The Canadian-income portion gives you income from Canadian companies. Income should be monthly and should be invested back in the fund(s). Remember, if you are taking out your income, you are losing growth opportunities on what you are taking out. The more you leave in, the faster it will grow. This return of income into the fund is known as the dividend-reinvestment option. Fund companies offer this without any additional cost. In stocks, dividend reinvestment is not as easy. This is one of the features I like in mutual funds.

The non-Canadian equity portion serves the same purpose as the Canadian version, but it can be global, international, regional or a combination.

The non-Canadian income portion serves the same purpose as the Canadian version, but it can be global, international, regional or a combination.

If you look at the world of investments as whole, Canada represents only 3%. Why then have I chosen Canadian investments as 50% of my portfolio? I believe in Canada, and I believe that many great companies exist on Canadian soil. Canada may represent only 3% of the world's investments, but our companies are doing business all around the world. I just would not be comfortable giving more than half of my investment dollars to non-Canadian companies.

If you think you would rather invest more internationally, just change your allocation to 40/60 or 25/75 or whatever fits your lifestyle. The easy portfolio is very flexible, so suit it to what you think is best.

In the next few pages, some examples will demonstrate different easy-portfolio configurations. These are just examples—I have not been paid by any fund companies to mention their names. I could not possibly list every possible portfolio; my examples are intended to help you understand how to pick your own funds. These are not recommendations.

Example: Canadian-Income Fund

Let me show you a Canadian-income fund that could fit in the Canadian-income segment of the easy portfolio. You can find a lot of information by looking at fund profiles on your fund company's Web site. A fund profile will tell you fund's investment objective, MER, top ten holdings, rate of return, asset allocation, geographic allocation, and so on.

Let's use the Scotia Canadian Income Fund as an example. How did I find this fund? I went to Scotia Bank's Web site (www.scotiabank.com) and looked for investment or mutual-fund links. Eventually, after clicking on a "mutual fund" link and a "fund category" link, I found the page for income funds. This page shows Scotia's income funds. I researched all of them and concluded that a Canadian income fund would best suit my needs. You can research any fund company's Web site in this manner. If you are not comfortable using the Internet, you can call fund companies and request a prospectus. The prospectus will have lots of information. Once you find a fund in the prospectus, you can request fund-specific literature. All of these documents are available for free.

Internet access is a must-have tool for investors. Internet access and computers are becoming more affordable, and you should not be without them. These tools will make your life a lot easier.

Example: Non-Canadian Equity Fund

Let's use a non-bank mutual fund this time. You will find lots of non-bank mutual fund manufacturers out there. Some of the well-known players are Fidelity, Templeton, AGF and CI. The problem is, these big guys are not licensed as brokers and won't be able to sell to you directly; you need to go through advisors, discount brokerages and dealers. I will discuss how to buy in a little while.

I researched the fund companies I just mentioned and chose CI Global Fund for my easy portfolio's non-Canadian equity section. I visited CI's Web site at www.ci.com, then clicked on Prices and Performance. This took me to a page listing funds by classes, so I chose the global-equity class and found CI Global Equity. I did same type of research with all other fund companies but decided to stick to CI Global after reading all the information provided on CI's Web site. It has the lowest MER among its peers, its volatility meter is not high, its geographic composition looks good and everything else provided appeals to me. In order to be a successful investor, you need to put in time and effort and educate yourself so you can make better decisions. When it comes to my money, only I care enough to make the best decision. I am definitely open to others' suggestions and ideas, but my final decisions will always be my own. No one else will realize the full value of my hard-earned money.

I am not going to discuss any more funds for the easy portfolio; I leave those choices to you once you complete your research.

Now I will show you steps that you can follow to start investing right away. Anyone can follow these simple procedures. You can invest on your own—or, if you think you are not ready to be on your own, I will show you guided options too. You just need to want to invest.

Chapter 12

Start Investing Now, Option A: Walk into a Bank

Walk Into a Bank

Walking into a bank is the easiest start for first-time investors. Just walk into the neighbourhood branch of your bank and go to the reception area or information desk. Tell the receptionist you would like to see a banker. Depending on what type of branch you are at, you may have to make an appointment for a future date.

Once you meet with your banker, you will be able to open an investment account and start investing right away. Bankers at your local branch are licensed to sell the bank's own mutual funds, GICs and so on, but they can't sell stocks or other investment products. These bankers can advise you on mutual funds; they are also known as mutual-fund specialists or mutual-fund representatives. Regardless of their title, these individuals can do business with you directly.

I like the idea of opening an account in my local branch for the following reasons.

- It's easy and simple.

- You will be filling out and signing a few forms while having a friendly conversation.

- Most banks offer front-end funds with zero commission—but always make sure that's what you are getting into.

- If you are not comfortable investing on your own, your banker will advise you at no cost.

- You can buy investments by taking out money from your checking or savings account in the same bank.

- Maintenance is easy. You don't need to worry about managing many accounts at different institutions.

Don't expect to find products from other institutions at your local branch. Let's say you are dealing with a Royal Bank branch; you can only purchase Royal Bank mutual funds at that location. If you would like to have both Royal Bank and TD Bank's mutual funds, you need to visit both of them. If you are looking for very simple investment solutions and don't want to go through the Internet, visiting banks is the option for you.

Miscellaneous

I walked into a CIBC branch in downtown Toronto in the summer of 2000. I had started my new job, and I had a check in my hand for a little less than $500. At that time, I was training to become an investment advisor, and I was not sure what to do with this small check. I had done some research on CIBC mutual funds, and I decided to invest in the CIBC Global Science and Technology Fund. When I met my banker, I told her that I had this $500 check, and I would like to buy this fund. She gave me a few forms to fill out, and her first question was, "Will this be a registered or non-registered account?"

Chapter 13

Start Investing Now, Option B: Make a Phone Call

Make a Phone call

Making a phone call is the middle ground between walking into a bank and using the Internet. You will not be able to get advice in person, but you will at least be speaking to a real person. All major Canadian banks employ licensed mutual-fund representatives. You can phone them and ask them to buy what you want. Also, if you want advice, these employees can provide it.

But before you call and buy, you need to open an account. To do this, either visit a branch and fill out some forms or call and ask the bank to mail the forms. Once you fill out these forms, mail them back, and your account will be ready. Completing these forms is a one-time thing; so is visiting the bank in person. You can buy and sell your favourite funds just by making a phone call. You can link your investment account with your bank account, so money can be taken from your bank account when you are making a purchase. Or you can keep money in a money-market type of fund and ask your mutual-fund representative to buy with money from that fund.

Option A and option B commingle. If you choose Option A, you will be able to exercise Option B, and vice versa. Also remember, as with Option A, that if you are calling Scotia Bank, don't expect to buy BMO mutual funds; you will only be able to purchase Scotia mutual funds.

I would like to discuss a Canadian mutual-fund company that might prove useful in exercising Option B.

Altamira is a Canadian mutual-fund company located in Toronto. It used to be an independent fund company, but it was bought out by National Bank in August 2002. In Canada, this is the only fund company that can sell directly to clients. You need only call to purchase funds from Altamira advisors; these advisors are licensed to advise and sell. Of course, if you don't want advice and only want to buy, you can do that too. I will give you phone numbers for major Canadian banks and Altamira in a separate chapter.

Chapter 14

Start Investing Now, Option C: Open a Trading Account

Open a Discount Brokerage Account

Opening a discount brokerage account gives you a lot more flexibility than any other options. You will be able to buy stocks, bonds, mutual funds and anything else if you choose this option. With one phone call from you, your trader can buy or sell any products for you. If you prefer not to talk to anyone, you can simply do everything online. All major Canadian banks offer discount brokerage services, and you need to shop for the most suitable one. I will give you phone numbers and Web addresses for five major discount brokerage dealers in Canada. These dealers are owned by major Canadian banks.

To exercise Option C, you need to open a trading account. You can call a discount brokerage firm to receive an application in the mail, or you can walk into any bank branch to get an application. Also, you can download an application online. Once your application is completed, mail it back or drop it off at the branch, and your account will be ready for trading within a few days. Remember, when you go to the branch to pick up an application, tell the person at the information desk that you would like to open an investment account or trading account.

Now, let me give you a few more necessary details.

Trading account: This refers to an open or non-registered account. A simple trading account usually comes in two different types:

Cash account: This is the type of account you should have. You pay in cash for all your transactions.

Margin account: Stay away from this type of account. Margin accounts let you buy investments on borrowed money. Buying investments with something you don't have can be a very risky business. Only professional traders, day traders, and aggressive investors buy on margin. I don't have a margin account, and I don't recommend one.

Registered account: You want this type of account if you would like to buy for your RRSP.

Registered accounts can be of two different types.

Self-directed RRSP: This type of account allows you to buy anything into your RRSP. You can have stocks, bonds, mutual funds and so on. This is just a registered version of the cash account. This type incurs an annual fee that can run from $50 to $100. I have this type of account for my RRSP. It gives me the option to buy anything I want in one place.

Basic RRSP: This is just a lighter version of the self-directed RRSP. The annual fee should be significantly lower than that of the self-directed RRSP, but you can only buy mutual funds in this account. If you are a first-time investor only looking to buy mutual funds, this type should be good enough for you. Don't pay more for services you don't need. Also, changing your account type is not a problem. Let's say you start with mutual funds. After five years, if you would like to explore the world of stocks, you just have to update your account type from basic RRSP to self-directed RRSP.

Your financial institution might not offer these exact same types of accounts. But once you know the basics and what you are looking for, you will be able to pick the right one for you. Option C will give you broader range of diversification and flexibility than Option A and Option B, but you must have Internet access. If you have Option C, you can buy anything at one place. You even can buy most of the mutual funds offered by major banks. Internet access makes your life a lot easier in every respect, not just in terms of investments.

If you have a discount brokerage account, you will be able to buy thousands of funds in one place—without paying any commission or transaction fees. To give you an example, TD Waterhouse offers over 1,750 no-fee funds. Also, you will be able to benefit from the advice of a mutual-fund specialist. This is a great feature for investors who are not comfortable choosing a fund by themselves. If you have Internet access, you will find hundreds of research tools to help you make informed and educated decisions.

In the next chapter, I will describe how you can filter these funds with the help of some free online tools. What do you need to use these tools? You know the answer. If you have Internet access, a computer, and time, you are ready to perform your own research.

Chapter 15

Cool Research Tools

The Wonder of the Web

The Web offers research tools for just about any topic; it's no wonder countless investment tools are among them. Most of these tools are free. Paid tools exist as well, but don't pay for something you can get for free. The three sites mentioned in this chapter offer lots of practical research tools. I mention only three sites because I do not want to bombard you with all these tools. Too much information can confuse people or scare them away, so I've kept it to a minimum.

Make these sites your friends and use them to research mutual funds or any other investment products. These sites are

   www.globefund.com
   www.moneysense.com
   www.morningstar.ca

www.globefund.com

Globefund.com is a part of Canada-based CTVGlobemedia—you know, those guys who run CTV and the *Globe and Mail* newspaper. Globefund.com, globeinvestor.com, globeandmail.com ... all of these sites are connected. You can switch back and forth by clicking on the menus on the top of each site.

Globefund.com mainly deals with mutual funds. You will find all sorts of mutual-fund news and market updates on this site. On the side, you will see bold menus like tracking tools, research tools, fund reports, resources and so on. Examine these menus and what they have to offer. Tracking tools allow you to track your portfolio, and you can create a fund list to watch. Once you have created your fund list or portfolio, the site will update it regularly.

Research tools are the best thing this site has to offer. These tools allow you to filter funds based on the information you input. You can specify the fund company, MER, load type, minimum investment and so on. Basically, you can view and choose funds that match your preferences. Another option you will see under Research Tools is the fund selector. You can select funds by inputting an asset class, fund company and so on. You will find a lot of other tools at this site, such as a tool to generate a chart from your fundlist or a tool to generate a report showing top moving funds. Discover these tools and play with them. Fund-report tools allow you to look up various reports and gain an overall picture.

You will find a lot of other tools at this site. Discover these tools and play with them. You will see what you can do with just a single click of your mouse. Everything is at your fingertips; you just have to make the most out of it.

www.moneysense.ca

I like *MoneySense* magazine, and their Web site, www.moneysense.ca, is worth mentioning. This all-Canadian site is so packed with features that visitors can become confused and overwhelmed. But if you know what you are looking for, this site can provide valuable resources.

You will see that this site offers lots of tools and articles. You can select these based on your interest, such as investing, mutual funds, tax, spending and so on. Take a look around; you will see lots of menus. I will describe the mutual-fund menu, but you can play with other menus as well.

Let's look at the My Money menu. You will see a tutorial, along with links back to home and to resources on investing, mutual funds, planning and so on. Click on the mutual-fund link to access that section of the site. Find the Mutual Fund Data heading. Under that heading you will find links to more fund data according to options such as

Mutual fund screener
Fund overview
Fund performers
Top funds
Bottom funds
Fund by performance ranking
Funds by family
Canadian equity funds
No-load funds

On the Web site, you will find many other options as well. Try all of them one by one or just choose those you need.

Mutual Fund Data isn't the only heading to explore. The Wrap, Index and Bond Funds heading is helpful as well. In this box, you will find a menu called More Fund Data. From that menu, you can choose options such as

Best mutual funds of last year
Canada's best fund families
How to spot a loser

These are only a few of the many options. Try all of them to research your funds. The MoneySense site has lot more features than I have just described. After you familiarize yourself with the site, you will be able to find what you are looking for right away. One thing you need to remember: by the time this book goes to press, all these menus and options might have changed. But don't be discouraged. The features and tools are still there somewhere; keep looking.

www.morningstar.ca

Morningstar is a U.S.-based company with operations in seventeen countries. The globally recognized company provides analysis, news and data on various investment products. Their Canadian site is located at www.morningstar.ca and can provide you with various tools and calculators. I also like the layout of this site.

I will not describe this site in detail, as the same ideas apply, and I am sure you will be able to manoeuvre through this site. My descriptions will not make any sense to you unless you visit the sites yourself. You will be surprised to see what can be done online. Every discount brokerage has its own site offering same kind of tools; try them all, and pick the one you like best for your research.

Five-Star Rating

You will notice that on Web sites, funds are often given a one-to five-star rating, with five stars being the best. Each site can explain how these ratings work. A full five-star rating does not necessarily mean "Jump into it!" Likewise, a one-star rating does not mean a fund is not worth looking into. Use these ratings as a tool and make your decisions based on your own research.

Chapter 16

ING Direct Mutual Funds

How Do ING Funds Work?

One fund company worth mentioning for first-time and do-it-yourself investors is ING Direct Mutual Funds. ING offers lots of options that can't be found anywhere else. ING offers funds from eight well-known Canadian fund families, and there is no minimum to buy. However, if you were to buy these same eight fund companies' funds through a discount brokerage or a broker, a minimum of $500 to $1000 would usually apply.

These eight fund companies are

- AIC
- Fidelity
- AGF
- FRANKLIN TEMPLETON
- BRANDES
- AIM TRIMARK
- CI Investments

- Mackenzie

Portfolio Funds

ING offers portfolio funds as well. Portfolio funds are funds of funds. ING portfolio funds are a mixture of the above-mentioned funds. You have to fill out ING's Risk Tolerance Questionnaire, and based on your score, you will be able to choose a conservative, moderate or aggressive portfolio.

Portfolio funds are cool, because they take away the guesswork behind choosing funds. Also, you can access funds from several fund companies in one place. This means less paperwork and fewer worries. One thing I don't like about portfolio funds is that you cannot change allocations of funds. If your chosen portfolio fund is made up of 35% Chinese funds, you don't get to change that percentage.

No Minimums, No Loads

ING offers no-load funds, which is a good thing for investors. I always ask you to make sure that you are not paying any fees and commissions, and ING funds offer just that.

Also, ING funds have no minimum requirement to buy. This is a unique feature; in Canada, you will not find any discount brokerage or mutual fund dealer offering it. Let me elaborate: ING portfolio funds and any funds from the eight fund companies mentioned have no minimum requirement to buy. You can start your account with any amount—as little or as much as you want. If you would like to start a PAC, the minimum requirement for ING portfolio funds is currently $100 per fund. There is no minimum to run a PAC from any one of the eight fund families listed.

How to Buy ING Funds

ING funds can be bought online or on the phone. Once you do your research and know what to buy, you can just pick funds from eight fund families or any portfolio funds. The ING Web site has a listing of all funds. If you are not sure what to buy, you can complete their Risk Tolerance Questionnaire. Based on your score, a portfolio fund will be recommended. I will give you ING's Web address and phone number at the end of this book. The Web site is easy to navigate; you can find the answers to all your questions. If you would like to talk to a live person, just call their toll-free number. ING mutual-fund specialists will answer your questions and guide you through the procedures to choose a fund, but they are not licensed to advise.

Miscellaneous

PAC stands for "pre-authorized checking." All fund companies allow you to run PAC weekly, biweekly, monthly, quarterly, semi-annually, and annually. PAC allows you to make systematic purchase in your account regularly. ING portfolios carry a PAC minimum requirement of $100, but the eight fund companies do not require a minimum. See chapter 7 for more info on PAC.

Chapter 17

Index Funds

What Are Index Funds?

Index funds are not actively managed funds. No portfolio managers run the fund. Index funds mirror the market performance of an index by buying stocks or other instruments that match the underlying index's composition.

The Idea

The idea behind an index fund is that it is not possible to beat the market by picking a few stocks. So instead of picking a few stocks, why not buy the whole market? Forget about beating the market, because now you *are* the market. Definitely not everyone agrees with this idea. Index funds offer unparallel savings opportunities to investors, because there are no active fund managers to pay.

Low MER

The MER for regular mutual funds can run from 1.5% to 4%, but the MER for index funds can range from .25% to 1%, which is significantly lower than regular mutual funds. In the long run, investors save lots of money on the MER.

TD e-Series Funds

In Canada, index funds are gaining popularity, and financial institutions are increasing their exposure. TD offers index funds for Canadian online investors, and these funds are called TD e-Series funds. (TD used to call these TD eFunds.) As far as I know, TD e-Series funds are the lowest-cost index funds in Canada. You can only buy TD e-Series funds online, and you need to have a TD e-Series funds account or TD Waterhouse Trading account to buy TD e-Series funds.

Miscellaneous

Index funds follow an index or indices. In a downward market, index funds will go down fast, because no active fund managers are working to eliminate the falling stocks. So choose only those index funds that meet your individual circumstances and investment goals.

Chapter 18

I Don't Have Money to Invest

Can I Still Invest with Limited Capital?

If you have managed to read this far, you must feel that my advice makes sense ... but that doesn't mean you have money to invest. It's just not you; non-investors always subscribe to the idea that investing is for other people—those with more money or knowledge.

Investment Is a Discipline

Investment is nothing but a discipline; it has to be orchestrated with great passion and care. Investment is not like going to the shopping mall and buying a few things impulsively. Start investing for the long run, and keep adding money every month or every week. Stay invested for the long run—through good and bad times, through market ups and downs. Research has shown that the stock market has averaged an annual 11% rate of return over the last 120 years. Cash has managed to return only 4% annually for the same 120 years. You will be surprised to know that stock markets actually have outperformed home values by a considerable margin in the long run.

Start with a Small Amount

You don't need a pocketful of cash to start investing. If you follow the procedures outlined in this book, you can open your first account with as little as $25—or even less. The hardest part is to start. Once you start, the rest will be a lot easier. If you think you can't gather $500 or $1000 to invest, start with a monthly plan and gradually increase your monthly contribution. Cut unnecessary expenses, such as

- Gym memberships you never use
- Frequent trips to fast-food restaurants
- Features on your home or cell phone you do not need

Cutting unnecessary expenses here and there should give you at least $25 to start a monthly PAC. If you are shy or worried about opening an account with a small amount, don't be. You earned that money, and any advisor should give you a thumbs-up just for planning for your future. The most important part is to start—and stick to it for the rest of your life. It takes your willingness and action to get started. So when you are starting—today, tomorrow or next week? The sooner, the better.

Miracles Happen When You Start Investing

Let's look at the scenarios of three individuals. One of them—we'll call him Mr. Early—starts investing at 20, with no initial deposit and with a $100 monthly PAC. Mr. Mid starts at

30, with no initial deposit and with a $100 monthly PAC, and Mr. Late starts at 40, with no initial deposit and with a $100 monthly PAC. If we assume an interest rate of 10% for each, and if everyone stops contributing at the age of 70, here are the results in approximate figures.

Mr. Early

Total deposit = $60,000
Growth = $1,400,000
Estimated value = $1,460,000

Mr. Mid

Total deposit = $48,000
Growth = $507,000
Estimated value = $555,000

Mr. Late

Total deposit = $36,000
Growth = $170,000
Estimated value = $206,000

Miscellaneous

When will you be a millionaire,

if you start with $1000
and make a monthly deposit of $100
with an interest rate of 10%?

It will take you **44 years** to be a millionaire. But if you consider 3% inflation, your one million dollars will be worth approximately $273,000 in today's dollars.

Chapter 19

Investment Scams: Use Common Sense to Protect Your Money

Why Research Matters

New investors are more vulnerable to many hundreds of investment—and money-related scams than veteran investors. Every few months, a new scam pops up, draining hard-earned money before it gets detected and publicized. Here I will describe a few of them; use common sense to protect yourself against these and others.

Telemarketing Calls

Always avoid buying or signing up anything over the phone, unless you initiated the call and are working with your trusted banker or other advisor. Licensed brokers or unlicensed reps may call and ask you to buy fraudulent stocks, worthless promissory notes, and high-risk penny stocks through high-pressure sales tactics. You may also receive calls from travel companies promising you a free trip or free dinner, utility companies offering one free month of service or free long distance and so on. Anyone looking to make a quick buck could also make a victim out of you.

The best course of action to protect yourself from telemarketing scams would be to subscribe to Caller ID and screen your calls with voice mail or an answering machine. If you don't recognize the phone number on your Caller ID, don't pick up. Urgent callers will leave a message. Telemarketers are trained to talk sweet and convince you to buy services or stuff you don't need. Sometimes it's hard to say no, even if you are aware of such telemarketing scams. That's why it's best not to pick up the phone in the first place.

If you do get stuck in a telemarketing situation, listen for these lines:

- I will double your money in two to three months.

- Fast in and fast out, and we'll put some money in your pocket.

- This is a ground-floor opportunity for you.

- If I make you money, you will be happy, right?

- We promise to match your investments.

- I am offering insider information to you only so you can make some money.

- I will double your money in two (or any other number) years.

- I am not going to let you down.

Internet Fraud

The Internet opens up endless scamming possibilities—no wonder con artists love it. Let's go over some major scams encountered in the last few years. Remember, new scams will arise every year; keep your eyes open.

Phishing: This is when con artists fish for your confidential information. You might receive authentic-looking e-mails from what appear to be your financial institutions or other well-known companies. These e-mails might state that your account had a large withdrawal or billing error. You will be prompted to click a link to update your account. That link will take you to a fake Web site that is almost identical to your bank or credit-card Web site. Once you update this fake site by entering your password, bank card or credit card number, and so on, your actual account will be emptied out. Yes, I know this is very scary and hard to believe. But every day, people fall for it and lose their life savings.

Trojan: A Trojan is a virus. It got its name from Greek mythology's Trojan horse. You can get this Trojan from chat rooms or via e-mail. In the chat room, con artists pretend to be a young girl trying to send you her pictures. Once you receive the pictures on your hard drive, the Trojan installs onto your computer. Also, you can get a Trojan virus via e-mail in a similar fashion. Now, what happens once a Trojan installs? The virus starts to track all of your computer activities, such as your keystrokes, e-mail, Internet activities and so on, then sends daily reports to the hackers who infected you with the virus. Basically, it's like someone put a video camera on top your computer and is watching your every move. This is how con artists get a hold of your personal information.

West African letter fraud: You meet a 20-something-year-old girl in a chat room. She sends you a few hot pictures. Then she mentions that her dad was a high-ranking government official or industrialist who left her millions of dollars. She explains that she is not able to move this fund from her dad's account due to regulations, and she needs your help. All you have to do is to give her your bank-account information to transfer her money out of the country; in return, she will give you 40 or 50% of her 10 or 20 million dollars. Wait, even more incentives remain. Since you are such a nice guy, she even would not mind spending a couple of months in a resort with you. You don't waste a second to grab this lifetime opportunity, handing over your banking information. A few days later, you find out that your bank account was emptied out. Your dream of spending quality time with a beautiful girl as a freshly minted millionaire is gone—and so is all the money in your bank account. Sometimes, the scammer claims to be from Nigeria, but it's always the same scam. Be aware.

Offshore investment scams: You receive promotional materials or bump into an advertisement. You are promised a high rate of return, free of taxes, because your dollars will be invested in an offshore location outside Canadian jurisdictions. Once you open your account and hand over your money, you never hear back again. These countries are well-known for offshore banking:

- Aruba

- Bahamas

- Cayman Islands

- Panama

Be extremely cautious when you are told to take shelter in offshore tax havens. Once your money leaves Canada, you are no longer under the protection of Canadian securities and banking laws. Also, if your money is gone, you will not be able to seek the help of Canadian authorities, because your original intention was to avoid taxes.

Penny stocks: Stocks that cost less than a dollar are called penny stocks. Most penny stocks trade over the counter or on junior exchanges, because these companies are not good enough to meet the standards of senior stock exchanges. You will always see online ads or newspaper ads about these penny stocks. These stocks are very volatile; price swings can happen frequently due to heavy promotion and market manipulation. Maybe one person in a thousand makes money out these stocks. Don't be a slave to your greed; penny stocks are perilous and should always be avoided.

The System: Let me give you an eternal stock-market tip that will remain true forever. **No one can predict the market.** Not I, not you, not any analysts, not Warren Buffett. Simply no one can or ever will. The System is a computer program that claims to do just that. It claims to tell you when to buy, when to sell, what to buy, what not to buy and so on, promising that if you follow instructions, you will be making thousands of dollars a day in ten minutes with one trade. You will find System ads on

TV, in newspapers, on the Net—basically everywhere. You will see the faces of happy people living their lavish lifestyles and offering glowing testimonies. You will see sailboats, sunny white sand beaches, palatial houses and expensive cars. These happy people will tell you how they are making thousands of dollars every day by using the System. Now let's look at the guy who invented the System. He is well dressed and very confident, having mastered the art of talking. These entrepreneurs are so nice that they will give you admission tickets worth hundreds of dollars to attend their seminars in your city for free. Wouldn't you like that?

OK. Enough is enough. Let's cut to the chase now. These systems use technical analysis and algorithmic models to predict the market. Maybe these predictions will succeed once in a while, but such predictions are impossible at a higher percentage. If you have basic knowledge of investments, chances are high that you will beat the System using your own analysis and prediction.

Just use common sense: if their system is so good and people can make so much money in ten minutes, why don't these brilliant guys stay home and make millions of dollars daily instead of doing seminars and selling their system across the country? I would just stay in the Bahamas and make buckets of money—wouldn't you? Once you attend their free seminars, you will leave a few hundred dollars poorer thanks to an irresistible limited-time offer (only for today) allowing you to buy their system at a lower price.

Tips

Here are some tips that should help you to deal with any kind of scam on a daily basis:

- Do not give out any financial or personal information in an e-mail or chat room.

- Be extremely careful when you open an e-mail with an attachment. Never click on any link or open any unknown attachment. If you don't recognize the sender, delete it right away. Your computer can become someone else's playground with a single click.

- If your e-mail program opens attachments automatically, turn off this feature. Check any documents for viruses before opening.

- If you do online banking or any money-related transactions, look for the "s" in your address bar. Your browser's address bar is where you type Web addresses (for example, http://www.adawn.net). Notice there is no "s" after "http" because you are not doing any money-related transaction on this site. If you open a bank Web site to log into your account, such as https://www.scotiaonline.scotiabank.com, you will see "s" right after "http." That "s" stands for "secure transaction." You will also be able to see a key or a padlock on the bottom of your browser, above your system tray. If you don't see the "s" or the key or padlock, leave that site and do not proceed with any financial transactions.

- Scam artists try to instill fear to get personal information. If you receive an e-mail saying your account will be terminated in 24 hours or that you have only 10 hours to claim this lottery money, or anything of a similar nature, do not reply to that e-mail. Instead, verify the proper authorities.

- Do not be intimidated by offers of lottery winnings or threats of legal action (because you visited this porno site, terrorist site or anything of this nature).

- Do not use your real name in a chat room. Do not give out your phone number and address to anyone.

- Do not download any files from anyone in a chat room.

- Do not click on any links from anyone in a chat room.

- Chat rooms are populated with scam artists. Be extremely careful when you chat with someone else. Don't believe everything others say. The worst scam I heard of dates back a few years. This has to be the dumbest one I have ever heard. Some guy from the U.S. met this beautiful girl in India. After seeing a few pictures and chatting with her online a few times, he fell for her, and she convinced him to send her money so she could fly to America to meet him. This guy actually sent her money, never to hear from her again. Concerned, he contacted local police, who then contacted Indian police. Indian police found out that those pictures he received were actually of a famous Indian actress, and the address she had given was a vacant apartment.

- Install a firewall on your computer. You can buy Norton, McAfee and so on, but these brand names can be costly. I find Zone Alarm to be very effective and economical. Some of my viruses never got detected by Norton, but Zone Alarm was able to find and kill them. Also, Norton slowed down my computer, but I never had any problem with Zone Alarm.

Use the firewall that suits you best. It's a must-have thing; if you have a computer, you need a firewall.

- Never buy any solicited investments. Hang up if someone tries to recommend you stocks or investments over the phone.

- If your broker or anyone else recommends investments with little or no risk, be extremely careful. Investments will always have risks.

- If it sounds too good to be true, most likely it is. Don't jump into anything without verification.

- If you believe you have been a victim or someone has tried to scam you, call PhoneBusters at 1-888-495-8501 or e-mail them at info@phonebusters.com. Visit their Web site at least once a month to keep yourself updated. PhoneBusters is a division of Ontario Provincial Police (OPP). Visit PhoneBusters at www.phonebusters.com

- Also, you can contact the Ontario Securities Commission (OSC) at 416-593-8314 or 1-877-785-1555 (toll free) or e-mail them at inquiries@osc.gov.on.ca. The OSC Web site is at www.osc.gov.on.ca.

- Remember, common sense and vigilance are your best defence. Always think your decisions through; avoid impulsive investments.

- Public securities filings and company or mutual-fund profiles are available at www.sedar.com. If you want to make sure a company or fund really exists, check that site.

Chapter 20

Tax and Investments

How Does Investment Taxation Work?

You pay taxes on your investments, although you are investing with earned money on which taxes have already been paid. It is a good idea to seek the advice of an accountant or a tax specialist. Due to the various tax implications, new investors simply can't be aware of all tax regulations. Tax rules change frequently, and you won't be able to keep up if you do not have a professional working for you. I will give you some tax basics in this chapter. Unless you are super-confident that you can handle investment-related tax issues, hire a tax person. Most likely, a tax professional has dealt with even the rarest issues many times before. Do not worry about the accountant fees; it pays off in the long run.

Let's go over how different types of investments are taxed. Understanding tax treatments for different types of accounts will save you money, and you will be steps closer to achieving your financial goals.

Non-Registered Plan

Non-registered accounts, whether it's your simple bank account or your trading account, are considered the same way for tax purposes by the Canada Revenue Agency (CRA). You pay taxes in three main ways:

Interest income: When you receive interest income from any source (such as a bank account, GIC, anything), you pay full taxes on that. The government does not give you any break or preferential tax treatment on interest income. It's just like paying taxes on your salary (tax payable at full marginal rate). If you are in the highest tax brackets, you can be paying almost 50% tax on interest income.

Capital gain/loss: Capital gain occurs when you sell your investments and receive more than you spent. Let's say you bought some stocks at $100 and sold them at $120. Your capital gain is $20. You can have a lot of gains (meaning the price has gone up a lot since you bought), but you don't pay any taxes as long as you don't sell them. Unsold gain is known as unrealized gain. When you sell, you realize your gain. You only pay taxes on realized gain.

But wait—you need to look for something else before you start paying taxes on your realized gain. Look for any investments in your non-registered or open account with realized losses. In other words, look for anything you sold for less than you paid to buy it. If you have a realized loss, you can use it to offset your realized gain, thus paying less tax on your realized gain. If your realized loss is more than your realized gain, you can carry this amount back three years or carry forward indefinitely to offset your gain.

Now, how do you pay taxes on realized gain? You pay taxes on 50% of your gain at the marginal rate. If you spent $100 to buy some shares and sold them for $200, your realized gain is $100. Fifty per cent of $100 is $50. You will be paying taxes on this $50 at your marginal rate.

Dividend income: Canadian taxation rules favour dividend income. Dividend from Canadian public corporations will have to be grossed up by 45% (in other words, you will have to include in your income a taxable dividend equal to 145%, instead of 100% of the dividend received). You will receive federal dividend tax credit, which is 19% of the grossed-up amount. Also, you will receive your own provincial tax credit. When you add up your federal and provincial tax credit, your tax rate on Canadian public companies will be about 18% to 32%.

The rationale for grossing up dividends and then giving a tax credit lies in the idea that the dividend-paying corporation has already paid tax (dividends are paid out of after-tax income) and that paid tax should be reflected at the shareholder level. Dividends from foreign companies are taxed as interest income, and dividends from private Canadian companies are still under the previous tax rates. Previously, the gross-up rate was 25%, and the dividend tax credit was 13.33% of the grossed-up amount.

Easy Examples

One simple example from each above-mentioned scenario will help you see the whole picture. Let's assume your marginal tax rate is 40%.

Taxes on capital gain:
You bought a stock at $100
You sold it at $150
Your capital gain: $150–$100 = $50
You pay taxes on half of your gain: 50% of $50 = $25
Your tax: 40% of $25 = $10
On a capital gain of $50, you pay the government $10 and keep $40.

Taxes on interest income:
This is quite straightforward. You pay tax at your marginal tax rate.
Your interest income: $50
Your tax: 40% of $50 = $20
On an interest income of $50, you pay the government $20 and keep $30.

Taxes on dividends:
You have received dividends from a Canadian public corporation: $50
Gross-up by 45%: $72.5
Federal tax credit: $72.5 × 19% = $13.77
Tax on grossed-up amount: 40% of $72.5 = $29
Your tax: $29–$13.77 = $15.23

Wait—that's not the end of it. You will also get your provincial tax credit, which will further reduce the tax you pay. I will give you an example for Ontario province. For other provinces, consult a tax professional.

Ontario announced an enhanced dividend tax credit, as follows:

Year	Dividend tax credit
2007	6.7%
2008	7%
2009	7.4%
2010 and beyond	7.7%

To make things simple, I will use the 2010 rate. If you are interested in any other years, just use the chart above.

Your Ontario province tax credit: $72.5 × 7.7% = $5.58

So if you are in Ontario in 2010, on a dividend income of $50, you will get a $13.77 federal tax credit and a $5.58 provincial tax credit.

Total tax credit: $13.77 + $5.58 = $19.35
Your tax: $29–$19.35 = $9.65
On a dividend income of $50, you pay the government $9.65 and keep $40.35.

Registered Plan

Now, stop for a moment and think about what I just have discussed regarding different types of tax treatments in a non-registered account. How about the same sort of transactions occurring in a registered account? What kind of tax issues you need to deal with? The answer is very simple: none. Yes, you read that right. If all of the above-mentioned situations occur in a registered account, you pay no taxes. You do not need to go through these calculations. You pay nothing at all. Capital gains, interest income or dividend income earned in a registered account are not taxable. You can buy, sell, switch products, earn interests and earn dividends, and you still pay no taxes. Only one condition applies here: all these activities have to be done within a registered account. You don't pay any taxes in a registered account. You don't pay taxes until you cash out your funds. This may not sound that great, but in the long term, a registered account can save you a lot of money.

The catch in a registered plan is that you pay withholding taxes when you take out money. How much tax will you pay? It depends on how much you are withdrawing. See the withholding tax rates under Miscellaneous in chapter 1. Another point to keep in mind: your withdrawal will be added to your income, and you will receive a T4RRSP tax slip.

A registered account is good as long as you are not withdrawing money. The government will allow you to withdraw money from your registered account at the end of the year in which you have reached 71 years of age. At that time, you have to convert your registered account to a registered income account.

Tax Tips

Follow these simple tax tips to maximize your returns. On my Web sites, you will find more tips and facts to help you become a better investor. I will discuss two Web sites I maintain for Canadians in the next chapter.

- If you are redeeming investments from your non-registered account, try to do it in the beginning of the year, such as in the month of January or February. By doing this, you can defer paying taxes almost one year, because you don't have to file income taxes for the current year until next year. If you redeem investments in November or December, you will be paying taxes in two to three months.

- You pay taxes on interest or dividends every year if you hold income—or interest-generating investments in a non-registered account. But if you hold the same investments in a registered account, you will not pay any taxes as long as you stay within the registered plan type.

- Withdrawing your investments or cashing out your money from a registered account hurts you badly with a one-two punch. You pay withholding taxes on your withdrawals, and it adds to your annual income. You then pay more taxes on your total income, and if you are just below the next tax bracket, the money you are withdrawing can put you over, which makes you pay a lot more taxes.

- If you have more capital losses than gains for the year (or if you have only capital losses but no gains), your excess capital losses (after offsetting gains, or just losses if you have no gains) can be carried back three years (to offset gains) or carried forward indefinitely to offset future capital gains.

- If you borrow money from a financial institution to buy a car or a house, your interest is not tax-deductible. But if you do the same to buy income-generating Canadian investments, your interest *is* tax-deductible. If you do not have funds to invest, but banks don't mind giving you loans, you can use this tip to create wealth. Before you start investing on borrowed money, you need to be aware of a few terms and conditions. I suggest you to talk to a tax specialist first.

- Investments inside an RRSP account accumulate tax-free, and this helps your investments grow faster. Consider opening an RRSP and starting a PAC if you can't contribute bigger amounts. After 20 or 30 years, you will be surprised to see what a $100 monthly PAC can do.

Chapter 21

Canada's Personal Finance Web Site

The Birth of Adawn.net

Mind Over Matters is my first Web site. This site offers lots of financial and some non-financial articles. When I started this site in 2006, I had no idea of how to run and maintain a Web site. At first, it really looked terrible. The layouts were bad, the colors did not coordinate and so on. But returning visitors mention that www.adawn.net looks a lot better now.

What Is This Site About?

I created this site to make personal finance easily accessible for Canadians. You can use lots of tools on the site to find various interesting facts, both financial and non-financial. Also, on some pages, I added stock-market charts that give you market updates and summaries. Let me walk you through some of the features on my site:

Financial tools: Some of these tools are

- Credit-card cost calculator
- Borrowing cost calculator
- Mortgage-saving calculator
- Mortgage-related tools
- Rent or buy Calculator
- Daily spending calculator

These are just a few examples; many more tools and calculators can be found on the actual page. Just click on the Financial Tools link.

Financial links: On this page, you will find links to other financial sites. I have chosen only the best resources. You can browse these sites to educate yourself at your leisure.

Travel tools: My Web site offers some interesting Canadian and international travel tools you never thought would exist. For instance, you can navigate the world's subways on one site, look up airline meals online, find free public toilets around the world and many other interesting things. I added this non-financial section to make your browsing experience more enjoyable.

Market Updates: You will find stock-market update charts and summaries in these sections: main page, personal-finance page, taxes page and world page. All these sections can be accessed from the main page at www.adawn.net.

Those are some of the tools you will find. My articles on various topics (some of them non-financial) can be found on the Archive page. New articles will be posted on the main page, in the left column. I would like to give you some examples of what kind of articles you can expect on my site. The following articles were posted on www.adawn.net and can still be viewed by going to the Archive section.

How Credit Cards Calculate Interest

Friday, April 27, 2007. Toronto. In Canada, credit-card companies use two methods to calculate the interest you pay. These methods are the average daily balance method and the daily balance method. Although the methods are different, they generate same interest charge. If you are interested in finding out which method your card uses, you can call their 800 number or find it in your credit card agreement brochure. Now let's look at these two methods.

Average Daily Balance Method

Your credit card has a billing period of 29 to 31 days. The average daily balance is just the average of your daily balance during your billing period. Average daily balance is calculated at the end of every month. Take the balance at the end of every day and add them up (A). Divide the total (A) by the number of days in your billing cycle to get average daily balance (B). B is multiplied by the daily interest rate to get the average daily interest amount (C). Now, to calculate your interest charge for the month, multiply C by the number of days in the billing period.

To get the daily interest rate, divide the annual interest rate by 365. Also, your interest rate can be found in your monthly statement.

Daily Balance Method

The daily balance method is simpler than the average daily balance method. Instead of making one calculation at the month's end, the daily balance method calculates your interest at the end of every day of the billing period. The calculation method is simple: multiply your daily balance by the daily interest rate, then add up the daily interest to obtain interest for the month.

Purchases, Cash Advances and Balance Transfers

If you pay your balance in full, you never pay any interest. If you don't pay your balance in full, you are charged interest from the date you made these purchases until they are paid in full. Some credit-card issuers charge interest from the date the purchases are posted to your account. You are charged interest from the date you made the cash advance or balance transfer.

Let Your Credit-Card Company Pay Your Interest

By paying your balance in full, you are actually using your card company's money for free for your billing period. Your card company always wants you to carry a balance, so they can charge you interest; that's how card companies make money. If you are paying your balance in full, you are actually using your card company's money at their high interest rate for free.

Let me give you an example. In September 2006, I bought five British Airways tickets at $2,000 each. My total cost was

$10,000 ($2,000 × 5). Most card companies charge a 20% annual interest rate. According to that rate, my one-month interest charge would have been $165. Yes, that's right: $165. But I avoided this charge by paying my balance in full. If you looked at this little differently, you could say that I borrowed money for one month at a 20% interest rate, but I have not paid any interest because my card company paid it for me.

Know how you are being charged and what your interest rate is. Pay your balance in full. It's like using your card company's money at their expense.

Minor RRSPs

Minors Can Have RRSPs

Friday, May 25, 2007. Toronto. There is no minimum-age requirement for opening an RRSP account. Children with any amount of earned income can invest. The following is required in order to do so:

- A SIN (social insurance number) is required for minors.
- Income has to be legitimate.
- Income has to be recorded with proper receipts or documents.
- T1 tax return has to be filed.

Advantages of an Early-Age RRSP

An early-age RRSP offers many advantages. The following are a few to mention.

- No actual contributions have to be made in the RRSP. Contributions can be made anytime later on. There is no time limit.

- Early investing accumulates RRSP room for several years, which can be carried forward indefinitely and increases lifetime contribution limits.

- The lack of an age requirement allows a minor to contribute in RRSP right after entering the workforce. Someone who did not contribute at an early age won't be able to contribute right after entering the workforce, because there will be no contribution room.

- RRSP deductions can be used anytime later on, when there is enough taxable income to use the deduction. There is no time limit to claim deduction.

- RRSPs give income-splitting opportunities to parents who own businesses. Parents can hire their own children as employees and can pay them accordingly. Give salary to a child as a tax-deductible business expense, and this will create contribution room for the child.

- Contributions made in the RRSP will start growing and compounding, tax-free, inside the plan.

- RRSPs are a great way to give children practical lessons about money and personal finance at an early age.

Minor RRSP Restrictions

Not all financial institutions allow minors to have an RRSP. Most of the banks and big fund companies (like CI Funds) will allow minors to open an RRSP. Some institutions might put restrictions on minors' accounts, such as

- A co-signer is required (fund companies can do this)
- Children can't invest in mutual funds (banks can do this)
- Children can only invest in GICs or savings accounts (banks can do this)

If you happen to face one of these or any other restrictions, do not get discouraged; just shop for the best one. A minor RRSP is a great investment vehicle for kids and can provide life-long benefits.

Other Articles

Here are some non-financial articles you will find on www.adawn.net. I will only mention titles. If you would like to read the full articles, please visit my Archive page.

> "Netvibes"
> "Lessons from a Third-World Country"
> "Canada's Arctic"

You can check daily for the latest financial and non-financial information. Visit www.adawn.net often; I am interested in your comments, suggestions and feedbacks. You can e-mail me from the site; click on the e-mail button on the main page, on the lower left side. I will discuss my other site, which is a blog site, in the next chapter. I will also mention the differences between a regular site and a blog site.

Chapter 22

A Dawn Journal

What Are Blogs?

A "blog" (short form of "Web log") is simply a log or journal or diary on the Internet. Years ago, when blogs first appeared, people usually wrote their daily events, thoughts, and ideas onto blog sites, but things have changed a lot since then. Now, blogs on a variety of subject are gaining popularity every day. Most of the famous authors and celebrities have their own blogs and update their sites on a regular basis.

What Are the Differences?

What are the differences between a regular Web site and a blog? Blogs connect authors with readers on a personal level, and blogs build lasting relationships that regular sites can't. You might be surprised to learn that my blog gained more popularity than my regular site just a few days after going live. I can talk about anything on my blog, including personal matters. On my regular www.adawn.net site, my writing is restricted; I need to maintain my site's professional presence.

A Journal Encompassing All Aspects of Life

You never know what type of articles you are going to read at www.adawnjournal.com. I update *A Dawn Journal* frequently, and I write on many subjects. Every time you visit, you will find something new and different. Here are the current categories under which I write on my blog. New categories are added if required.

> Canada
> Current events
> Health
> History
> Internet
> Life
> Movie reviews
> Personal finance
> Smart tips
> Toronto

Sample Postings

You Are Free

If you happen to live in Alberta, British Columbia, Ontario or Quebec—starting March 14, 2007, you are allowed to change your wireless carriers without changing your phone number. The rest of the provinces will be able to do the same by September 12, 2007. Previously, you were not able to take your cell phone number with you if you decided to leave your carrier. The CRTC (Canadian Radio-television and Telecommunications Commission) lifted the restriction to attract fierce competition, thus benefiting subscribers with more selection and lower pricing.

It did not take long for a new player to enter the Canadian market since the launch of MNP (mobile number portability). On the same day, Amp'd Mobile—a U.S.-based carrier—started their operations in Canada. Amp'd is the first foreign carrier to enter Canada. I am sure there will be a lot more in the upcoming years. I hope all these translate into something very simple for Canadians: lower phone bills and better customer service. Canadian cell phone rates are one of the highest among all industrialized nations, and it should end soon. Check the Amp'd Mobile Web site at www.ampd.ca.

Original version posted on Wednesday, March 21, 2007, at 11:11 p.m. by A Dawn in Smart Tips

Don't Throw Out Your Credit Cards Yet—First, Pick Up Your Phone

Yesterday, I decided to get rid of two credit cards. These two cards had been in my wallet for so long, and I never used them. As I was calling customer service to close my account, my friend suggested just throwing out my cards. He said he never bothers to call, because it is a waste of time. Many of us do the same thing. A lot of us don't realize that if you do not call your card company and close your account, your account will remain active, and it will appear on your credit report as a credit.

So if you opened accounts here and there years ago just to get a 10% discount and forgot about it, that's probably what is making your credit report lengthy. We don't know how many credit cards we have, and all these accounts appear on our reports. Creditors may not like the appearance of so many accounts. So before you throw out your credit card next time, make sure you pick up the phone and call your credit-card company to close your account first.

Original version posted on Wednesday, March 28, 2007, at 11:15 p.m. by A Dawn in Personal Finance

Green Tea

You must have noticed the steady stream of news regarding the health benefits of green tea. Studies show that green tea can cut cancer risks, lower your blood pressure, protect you from Parkinson's and Alzheimer's disease, make your heart healthy and do a lot more that we do not know about yet. I knew about all these benefits, but this knowledge did not motivate me enough to make green tea part of my daily routine until now.

A recent study found that in addition to all known benefits, green tea can even fight against HIV. The secret lies in a component called EGCG, which fights to keep HIV from taking control of the immune system. Drinking green tea may lower the risk of HIV and also could slow down the spread of HIV. Although more research is needed, this is enough for me to start drinking green tea. I am sure similar news will come out in the future, and there is no need to wait for any conclusive reports. I will start drinking green tea today, and it will be one of my lifetime healthy habits.

Original version posted on Saturday, March 31, 2007, at 12:18 a.m. by A Dawn in Health

Double Your Money

Have you ever looked at your savings-account statements and wondered how long would it take to double your money at the interest rates mentioned on those statements? By using a simple formula, you will be able to figure this out very quickly.

This simple formula is called the Rule of 72. The rule works when your interest rate is compounded annually and you are not taking out any money or interests from your account. To find out how long it will take to double your money, divide 72 by your interest rate. Yes, 72 is the magic number here. Let's say your high-interest savings account is paying you 3% interest. Divide 72 by 3, and you get 24 years. If you add more money every month to your capital, your money will double in fewer years. If you have a mutual fund that returns roughly 10% annually, your money will double in 7.2 years. Don't be discouraged by these long years. Investment is a discipline, and you should not expect miracles to happen overnight

Original version posted on Monday, April 16, 2007, at 08:11 p.m. by A Dawn in Personal Finance

What Is Web 2.0?

"Web 2.0" does not refer to any new or updated version of the Internet. "Web 2.0" is just a phrase or term for recent Internet usage trends. Tim O'Reilly, founder of O'Reilly Media, started this term, and now it is widely popular and widely used.

"Web 2.0" refers to a new kind of Web. The Web has evolved so much that now it is an indispensable part of our lives. We use it daily to do stuff like social networking, gathering information, organizing events, sharing our calendar, etc. So

Web 2.0 refers to a changed Web that is now an integral part of everyday living. Some examples of Web 2.0 would be blogging, Google Calendar, Wikipedia, Netvibes and so on.

Original version posted on Monday, April 30, 2007, at 9:10 p.m. by A Dawn in Internet

Deposit 50 Cents to Make a Phone Call

The Canadian Radio-television and Telecommunications Commission (CRTC) has decided on new pricing rules for Canadian local phone services. As a result of these new rules, starting June 1, 2007, pay-phone calls could cost you 50 cents per call. Non-cash calls, such as credit-card or charge calls, could go up as high as $1 per call. These calls currently cost half the proposed amount in most parts of Canada.

These increases will definitely not affect the CRTC policy analysts or phone-company employees, because it is unlikely that the people behind these changes ever need to use pay phones. Although the use of cellular phones has skyrocketed in recent years, Canada has not seen any cell-phone rate cuts like some other industrialized nations. Minimum-wage earners, students and many others are far from receiving the benefits of cell phones; the pay phone rates hike will affect these people. Bell has not changed its rates since 1981; now, the CRTC is basically allowing Bell and other phone companies to charge as they wish. If money is desperately needed (although I doubt it), a $.25 call could be increased to 35 cents (as Telus did in Alberta a decade ago), which is more sensible than doubling it. Obviously, these rulings represent the interests of phone companies, not the interests of general population.

Original version posted on Wednesday, May 2, 2007, at 08:10 p.m. by A Dawn in Canada

Keeping You Updated

The above should give you an idea of my blog content. Reading this site will keep you updated on various topics from a Canadian perspective. Check *A Dawn Journal* at www.adawnjournal.com often and make it your regular habit.

Afterword

Easy Steps

We have gone through the basic concepts of investing; by now, you should have a clear understanding of what steps to follow while investing for the first time. In this chapter, I will summarize the steps or procedures you need to take to start investing.

I will divide the whole scene into two categories: one for investors who would like to start on their own, and one for investors who would like to seek the help of a financial specialist.

I Am Not Ready to Invest on My Own

Over the Phone

Decide whether you would like to receive advice over the phone or in a face-to-face conversation. If you don't mind getting everything done over the phone, you can call a mutual fund specialist, as I described in chapter 13. You can pick any bank that offers mutual funds, or you can go with Altamira. Check the resources at the end of this book for the phone numbers of major players in the Canadian market.

Face-to-Face

If you would like to meet the person you are dealing with, the only option you have is talking face-to-face. In order to do this, you have to walk into your local branch, as I mentioned in chapter 12. You might also be able to meet an Altamira advisor; call Altamira to check if they are available in your area.

Etc.

You don't have to worry about what type of account you should open, what funds to choose or what research to conduct if you are talking to an advisor. However, this does not mean that you have to go by everything an advisor says. You can pick your own funds, choose your own account type and so on while still working with an advisor. It's your money, and only you should make the final decisions. If you don't want something, by law, your advisor must respect your wishes. Also, you cannot buy products from other institutions if you are seeing an advisor at your local branch.

I Am Ready to Invest on My Own

If You Have Internet Access

Follow these steps to start investing on your own.

- Choose your account type (chapter 1).
- Decide where you would like to open your account. Your options include at your local bank branch, at a bank that is not your local branch, at ING Direct, at a discount brokerage and so on (chapters 12, 13 and 14).

- Pick your funds. Do your research to help you choose. Use the tools mentioned in chapter 15. You can pick one fund or more than one. If you are investing small amount, such as $25 a month PAC (chapter 18), you have no option but to invest in one fund. If you are investing a larger amount, you should have more than one fund to diversify. The easy portfolio (chapter 11) is an example that shows you how to allocate your funds to achieve diversification. You can easily create your own portfolio based on your own needs. Some readers may like to hold 50% equity and 50% income funds, some may like mostly equity funds and some may prefer all income funds. Another option you have to diversify your investments (even if you are doing only a $25 monthly PAC) would be to use portfolio funds (funds of funds) made by fund companies. An example is ING Direct Portfolio Funds (chapter 16). The ING Web site can be a great tool for choosing funds, if you are not sure what to pick. You have to fill out a Risk Tolerance Questionnaire; based on your score, you will be given a portfolio to pick.

- Pick up or download an application on the net, or call customer service to obtain an application (chapters 12, 13 14).

- Fill out your application properly. If you are stuck on a question or not sure about anything on the application, call customer service and ask them to help you. Don't be shy or reluctant to call.

- Submit your completed application. You can mail it back or drop it off at a branch (chapters 12, 13 14).

- Your account should be ready in a few days. Depending on the institution you are dealing with, it can take anywhere from one to three weeks. You can ask customer service to give you an approximate time frame if you are dying to know.

- Start investing. You can invest by walking into a branch, by picking up your phone, or by typing on the Net, based on what type of account you have.

If You Don't Have Internet Access

I do not recommend this option. You should choose this option only when you absolutely can't access a computer. Investment procedures are basically as above, except you have to pick your fund differently. You can't do your research using the hundreds of tools available online; you will have to gather information manually.

Call each of the fund companies or financial institutions I have mentioned under Resources. If you require more fund company names, pick up a copy of the daily newspaper. In the business section, you will see lots of fund companies. Call them and ask for a prospectus and annual report, then review this literature. This can be a laborious task, and it might not work for you. If you have no Internet access, walking into a branch or dealing with bank fund companies or companies like Altamira would be a lot easier and would make sense. Pick what you think fits you most and works out best for you.

Conclusion

A Wonderful Journey

It is hard to believe, but we are in the closing chapter of this book. I enjoyed every moment of writing it, and I hope you enjoyed every moment reading it. I have tried my best to write this book in simple and understandable terms, so you don't need to look for a financial dictionary while reading it. Reading this book will definitely broaden your knowledge, but it will not do you any good unless you start taking action. Once you finish reading this book, you can put it on your shelf and forget about it after a couple of days ... or you can start taking action to change your life. I will consider my work successful if this book can make you determined enough to change and improve your life by taking positive action toward your financial goals.

Where Do We Go from Here?

Investment is not a miracle. Investment is a discipline. You need a plan, and in order to be a successful investor, you have to stick to your plan for the long run. Don't expect to see results overnight, and don't expect to become a millionaire in a year by trading risky stocks. Don't worry if you are starting with a small amount. The most important part is to start. Start with whatever amount you are comfortable with, and gradually increase your contributions.

Write It Down

I have added some blank pages at the end of this book. Use those or your own journal to write down your investment objectives or goals, including the procedures you would like to follow to achieve them. Write down every detail. Once every six months or once a year, go through your journal and your portfolio to see how you are doing and whether you need to change anything to reach your investment goals.

Emotion and Risk

Money and investing are emotional matters, and emotionally driven decisions can be risky. Don't be an emotional investor. Avoid unnecessary risks by not making emotional decisions. Emotional investing can be a recipe for disaster.

Try to minimize risk from all angles. Nothing is certain when it comes to investing, and you can take steps to reduce risk. Based on your risk tolerance, find suitable funds and monitor your funds to make sure investment objectives are met consistently. A simple but powerful method to minimize risk is to use a diversified portfolio. You can construct your own portfolio using the guidelines provided in this book, or you can use premade portfolio funds provided by fund companies.

Avoid Market Timing

Don't try to time the market. Chasing the market is a risky business and may cost you your whole portfolio. No one can predict the market, which will always have ups and downs. Focus on your long-term goals. Start investing, keep adding money, and stay invested. If you start early, you will have time on your side; even a smaller amount will turn into a large amount in the long run. Some market gurus claim that market timing works, and that they have been successful doing it. I will believe such claims the day I become psychic. But for now, I don't have the ability to see what the future holds. I don't believe in market timing, and I don't recommend it.

Feedback

Feedback is always welcome. Your opinions matter, and I would like to hear them. Communication fosters a connection between readers and author. Let me know if this book worked out for you—or even if it didn't. Let me know which parts of this book you find most helpful and which parts you think did not help and/or need more elaboration or clarification. Based on your feedback, I will update the future edition.

How to Contact Me

The easiest way to contact me would be to send me an e-mail. My e-mail address is adawn.net@gmail.com. Also, you can contact me by leaving a comment on my blog; I will reply right below your comments. If you would like to write me a letter in the traditional way, you can use my publisher's address, and it will reach me.

The Journey Is the Destination

Readers like you inspired me to write this book. I thought I would share valuable knowledge and hopefully change someone else's life. I believe in what I said, and every word in this book came out spontaneously. I enjoy writing for you, and my journey has taken me to my next trip: my second book. I have not decided yet what the name will be, but *Save Now* seems to be a good option at this moment.

You will encounter many money-saving tips in your life. In my next book, I will be writing about some of the tips you can follow to save money every day, month after month. I will start working on my second book shortly after this book is published.

I hope to see you again, and until then, remember: live for the journey, not for the destination. The journey *is* the destination.

Resources

Where Can I Get Information?

This section is simply a list of the phone numbers and Web addresses of those fund companies, banks and discount brokerages I have mentioned in this book. Also, I will add some personal finance and news sites, so you can broaden your knowledge. I have thought about this chapter throughout the course of writing this book, and I have decided to keep this list minimal, so you will not get overwhelmed. If you would like to explore more resources, feel free to visit www.adawn.net/financiallinks.html.

Resources

Mutual Funds

    AGF
    www.agf.com
    1-800-268-8583

    ALTAMIRA
    www.altamira.com
    1-800-263-2824

    AIM TRIMARK

www.aimtrimark.com
1-800-874-6275

CI FUNDS
www.ci.com
1-800-563-5181

FIDELITY
www.fidelity.ca
1-800-263-4077

FRANKLIN TEMPLETON
www.franklintempleton.ca
1-800-387-0830

ING DIRECT
www.ingdirect.ca
1-877-700-1737

Bank Mutual Funds

BMO MUTUAL FUNDS
www.bmo.com/mutualfunds
1-800-665-7700

CIBC MUTUAL FUNDS
www.cibc.com/ca/mutualfunds
1-800-465-3863

RBC FUNDS
www.rbcfunds.com
1-800-769-2599

TD MUTUAL FUNDS
www.tdcanadatrust.com/mutualfunds
1-866-222-3456

SCOTIA MUTUAL FUNDS
www.scotiabank.com (click on Mutual Funds under the Investing header)
1-800-268-9269

Discount Brokerages

BMO INVESTORLINE
www.bmoinvestorline.com
1-888-776-6886

CIBC INVESTOR'S EDGE
www.investorsedge.cibc.com
1-800-567-3343

RBC DIRECT INVESTING
www.rbcdirectinvesting.com
1-800-769-2560

TD WATERHOUSE
www.tdwaterhouse.ca
1-800-465-5463

SCOTIAMCLEOD DIRECT INVESTING
www.sdbi.com
1-800-263-3430

Financial Sites—Canadian Perspective

CBC MONEY
www.cbc.ca/money

GLOBEINVESTOR
www.globeinvestor.com

MONEYSENSE
www.moneysense.ca

YAHOO CANADA FINANCE
www.ca.finance.yahoo.com

International News and Financial Sites—Global Perspective

FORBES
www.forbes.com

INTERNATIONAL HERALD TRIBUNE
www.iht.com

THE ECONOMIST
www.economist.com

Investor Educational Sites

INVESTOPEDIA
www.investopedia.com

INVESTORED
www.investored.ca

MONEYCHIMP
www.moneychimp.com

Fund-Resource Sites

GLOBE FUND
www.globefund.com

MORNINGSTAR CANADA
www.morningstar.ca

MONEYSENSE
www.moneysense.ca

THE FUND LIBRARY
www.fundlibrary.com

Newspaper Financial Sites

TORONTO STAR BUSINESS
www.thestar.com/business

CANOE MONEY
www.money.canoe.ca

Government of Canada Sites

MONEY TOOLS
www.moneytools.ca

CONSUMERS AFFAIRS
www.consumer.ic.gc.ca

ONTARIO SECURITIES COMMISSION
www.osc.gov.on.ca

PUBLIC SAFETY
www.safecanada.ca

PHONE BUSTERS
www.phonebusters.com

Notes

Notes

Index

Altamira, 60
Asset-backed bonds, 25

Back-end loads, 41
Balanced funds, 49
Blogs, 103
Bond funds, 46–47
Bonds
    debt investment, 23
    definition of, 23
    face value, 24
    interest rates/coupon, 24
    an investment product, 23
    market value, 24
    par value, 24
    and stocks, 22–23
    types of, 24–26
    yield, 24
    YTM, 24
Bond types
    corporate, 25
    government, 25
    municipal, 26
    zero-coupon, 26

Callable bonds, 25
Canada Revenue Agency (CRA), 3
Canada's personal finance Web site
    Adawn.net, 96
    articles posted on, 98–102
    financial links, 97
    financial tools, 96–97
    market updates, 97
    travel tools, 97
Canadian Deposit Insurance Corporation (CDIC), 35
Canadian equity funds, 40, 52
Canadian income funds
    defined, 52
    example of, 53–54
Canadian investment Web research tools
    five-star rating, 69

www.adawn.net, 96–102. See also Canada's personal finance Web site

www.globefund.com, 65–66

www.moneysense.ca, 66–68

www.morningstar.ca, 68

www.sedar.com, 44

Canadian mutual-fund companies

    Altamira, 60

    ING Direct Mutual Funds, 70–72. See also ING Direct Mutual Funds

    Morningstar, 68

Cash accounts, 62

Cashable GIC, 27

Closed-end funds, 45–46

Common stocks, 22

Convertible bonds, 25

Corporate bonds, types of, 25

Dawn, A.

    blogs defined by, 103

    difference between Web site and blog, 103

    life aspects discussed by, 104

    journal of, 103–109

    sample postings by, 104–109

Debentures, 25

Deferred sales charge (DSC), 41

Deferred tax, 6

Discount brokerage account, 61

Dividend income, 90

Dividend-reinvestment fund, 52

Dollar-cost average, 31

Dow Jones Industrial Average (DJIA), 18

Electronic markets, 13–14

Equity funds, 46

Escalating-rate GIC, 27

Ethical funds, 47

Face value, 24

Fees and expenses

    avoiding mutual funds, 38

    concept of loads, 40–41. See also Loads and mutual funds

    definition of, 37–38

    MER, 38–40. See also Management expense ratios (MER)

    mutual fund prospectus, 42–43

    and mutual funds, 35

    trailer, 42

Financial instruments, 13. See also Financial products

Financial markets

    definition of, 12

    electronic, 13–14

physical, 13–14
and stock exchanges, 13–14. See also Stock exchanges
Financial products
   bonds, 23 See also Bonds
   defined, 21
   guaranteed investment certificate (GIC), 26–27
   stocks, 22–23
First-time investors
   and dollar-cost averaging, 31
   mutual funds suitable for, 28–29
   starting with investments, 56–58
Fixed-income funds, 46–47
Front-end loads, 40–41
Fund companies
   mutual funds and, 33
   and portfolios, 51–55
   trailer fees and, 42
Fund of funds, 51
Fund managers
   described, 28
   and professional management, 31–32
Funds
   closed-end, 45–46
   dividend-reinvestment, 52
   equity, 46
   ethical, 47
   global, 49
   income, 46–47
   international, 49
   money-market, 47
   non-Canadian equity, 52–53
   open-end, 45–46
   regional, 47
   sector, 47
   segregated, 48, 50
   specialty, 48

General-obligation bonds, 26
GIC. See Guaranteed investment certificate (GIC)
Government bonds, 25
Growth-fund managers, 46
Guaranteed investment certificate (GIC)
   cashable, 27
   defined, 26
   escalating-rate, 27
   index-linked/market-linked, 27
   and saving accounts, 27

Income
   Canadian, 52–54
   defined, 5
   dividend, 90

funds, 46–47
interest, 89
non-Canadian, 52–54
Income funds, 46–47
Index funds
defined, 73
low MER, 73–74
TD e-Series funds and, 74
Index-linked GICs, 27
Indices, 19
and base level, 17
defined, 16
relation to stock exchange, 16–17
world's major, 17–19
Inflation
defined, 8
effects of, 8
and investments, 9
measurement of, 8
ING Direct Mutual Funds
buying, 72
no-load funds, 71
PAC and, 72
portfolio funds, 71
working of, 70–71
Initial public offering (IPO)
defined, 13
issuing, 13–14

Interest income, 89
Interest rates/coupon, 24
Internet frauds
market status and, 83–84
offshore investment scams, 82–83
penny stocks, 83
phishing, 81
Trojan, 81–82
West African letter fraud, 82
Investment options
making phone call, 59–60
opening discount brokerage/trading account, 61–63
walking to nearest bank, 56–58
Investment resources
bank mutual funds, 120–121
discount brokerages, 121
financial sites, Canadian perspective, 122
financial sites, global perspective, 122
fund-resource sites, 123
government of Canada sites, 123–124
international news, global perspective, 122
investor educational sites, 122–123
mutual funds, 119–120

newspaper financial sites, 123
Investments
  discipline and, 75–76
  important resources for, 119–124
  important tips while making, 115–118
  and inflation, 9. See also Inflation
  limited capital and, 75
  and mutual funds, 9, 28–29. See also Mutual funds
  open/non-registered accounts and, 1
  opening an account, 1, 6
  registered accounts and, 1
  and scams, 79–87
  simplified, 10–11
  starting with small cash, 76
  steps to start making, 111–114
Investment scams
  avoiding telemarketing calls, 79–80
  important tips for avoiding, 85–87
  and internet fraud. See Internet frauds
  necessary to research, 79
Investment taxation
  examples of, 91–92
  non-registered plan, 89–90
  registered plan, 93
  tips to maximize returns, 94–95
  working of, 88
IPO. See Initial public offering (IPO)

Large-cap funds, 49
Loads and mutual funds, 40–41

Management expense ratios (MER), 35
  concept of, 39–40, 43
  definition of, 38–39
  index funds and, 73–74
  and NAV, 39–40
Market-linked GICs, 27
Market value, 24
Market value/capitalization method, 14
  NASDAQ Composite, 18–19
  S&P/TSX Composite Index and, 17–18
MER. See Management expense ratios (MER)
Mid-cap funds, 49
Money-market funds, 47
Municipal bonds, 26
Mutual funds, 9
  advantages of, 30–34

Canadian equity, 52
Canadian income, 52
custodian and, 33
definition of, 28
disadvantages of, 35–36
for first-time investors, 28–29
fund companies and, 33
key points, 33
large-cap, 49
mid-cap, 49
professional management and, 31–32
prospectus, 42–43
small-cap, 49
Mutual funds, advantages
    diversification and convenience, 32
    liquidity, 34
    low minimums and PAC, 30–31
    professional management of funds, 31–32
    regulating funds, 32–33
    transaction costs, 34
Mutual funds, disadvantages
    fees and expenses, 35
    holding cash, 36
    loss of controls, 36
    provision of insurance, 35
    trading limitations, 36

NASDAQ Composite, 18–19
National Association of Securities Dealers Automated Quotations (NASDAQ), 16
Net asset value (NAV), 39–40, 43
New York Stock Exchange (NYSE), 15
Non-Canadian equity funds
    defined, 52–53
    example of, 54–55
Non-registered accounts, 1. See also Open accounts
    capital gain/loss, 89–90
    dividend income, 90
    interest income, 89
Non-registered plan, 89–90. See also Non-registered accounts

Offshore investment scams, 82–83
Open accounts, 1–2
Open-end funds, 45–46

PAC. See Pre-authorized checking (PAC)
Par value, 24
Penny stocks, 83
Physical markets, 13–14
Portfolio, 49
    diversification in, 51
    easy and simple, 52–53

Pre-authorized checking (PAC), 72
defined, 31
and dollar-cost averaging, 31
low minimums and, 30–31
Preferred share, 23
Price-weighted method
defined, 14, 19
Dow Jones Industrial Average and, 18

Realized gain, 89–90
Rear-end loads, 41
Regional funds, 47
Registered accounts, 1, 62
advantages of, 3
basic registered retirement savings plan (RRSP), 63
deferred tax, 6
disadvantages of, 3–4
self-directed RRSP, 62
Registered income fund (RIF), 3–4
Registered plan, 93
Registered retirement savings plan (RRSP), 2–3. See also Registered accounts
annual limit, 4
basic, 63
minor, 100–102
self-directed, 62
Revenue bonds, 26

RRSP. See Registered retirement savings plan (RRSP)

S&P/TSX Composite Index, 17–18
Saving accounts
disadvantages of, 7, 9
flaws in, 8
and guaranteed investment certificates (GICs), 27
inflation and, 8. See also Inflation
and investments, 9
Sector funds, 47
Segregated funds, 48, 50
Small-cap funds, 49
Specialty funds, 48
Standard and Poor's 500 (S&P 500), 18
Stock exchanges
and base level, 17
defined, 13
major, 15–16
market value/capitalization method, 14
measuring, 14
price-weighted method, 14
world's largest, 14–15
Stock market indices, 16
Dow Jones Industrial Average (DJIA), 18
NASDAQ Composite, 18–19

　　　　other indices, 19
　　　　S&P 500, 18
　　　　S&P/TSX Composite Index, 17–18
Stock markets
　　　　defined, 12
　　　　and financial instruments, 13
Stocks
　　　　and bonds, 22–23
　　　　common, 22
　　　　defined, 22
　　　　as investment product, 22
　　　　preferred shares, 23

Tax
　　　　deferred, 6
　　　　and investment, 88–95. See also Investment taxation
　　　　savings, 5
　　　　withholding, 5

TD e-Series funds, 74
Toronto Stock Exchange, 15
Trading accounts, 1, 61–63
Trailer chart, 44
Trailer fees, 42
Treasury bills, 25
Treasury notes, 25
TSE 300 Composite Index, 17
Turnover ratio, 42

Unrealized gain, 89

Value managers, 46

West African letter fraud, 82

Yield, 24
Yield to maturity (YTM), 24

Zero-coupon bond, 26

978-0-595-46132-5
0-595-46132-8

LaVergne, TN USA
02 March 2010
174706LV00007B/132/P